A COLLECTION

OF

TEMPERANCE DIALOGUES

FOR

DIVISIONS OF SONS, GOOD TEMPLAR LODGES,

SECTIONS OF CADETS, BANDS OF HOPE, AND

OTHER TEMPERANCE SOCIETIES.

COMPILED BY

S. T. HAMMOND, D.G.W.C.T.

OTTAWA:
PUBLISHED BY S. T. HAMMOND.
HUNTER, ROSE & COMPANY, PRINTERS.
1869.

CONTENTS.

CONTENTS.

Temperance Dialogues.

MARRY NO MAN IF HE DRINKS:
OR,
LAURA'S PLAN AND HOW IT SUCCEEDED.

DRAMATIS PERSONÆ.

LAURA BELL...A Reformer.
SUSIE GRAY, }
NETTIE ELLIS, } ....Laura's Friends.
MORRIS HALL, }
WILL. BURNSIDE, } ....Admirers of these Ladies.
FRED. ALLEN, }

SCENE I.

PARLOR.—LAURA *sitting by a table, her head resting on her hand, as if in deep thought;* NETTIE *sewing;* SUSIE *reading. All silent for a few moments.*

LAURA.—[*Raising her head and speaking with emphasis.*] I have it, girls! I have it!

SUSIE.—[*Jumps.*] Oh, my! how you have startled me! What *have* you got, Laura—a fit?

LAURA.—No—an idea, and a plan.

NETTIE.—Wonderful!

SUSIE.—Astonishing!

NETTIE.—Shall we be honored with the development

of this brilliant inspiration? or is it too profound for our untaught minds to comprehend?

LAURA.—Now, girls, *do* be serious, for I am in sober earnest, and what I wish to say is the result of long and anxious thought.

SUSIE.—Mercy on me, how solemn! but, as they say in meeting—"Sister Bell will please proceed." [*Closes her book.*] Put away your sewing, Nettie. Now, Laura, you have our profound attention.

LAURA.—Very well. Now assist me, if you please, to call to mind the young men of our immediate circle of acquaintance who use intoxicating liquors; also those who use tobacco.

SUSIE.—Oh! I like to talk about the beaux. I caught two splendid ones at the skating park last night—but I forgot—we're to be serious. [*Puts on a long face.*]

LAURA.—Let me see. There's George Boswell—smokes. Ed. Stacy—smokes, chews, and drinks occasionally.

NETTIE.—John West—does he smoke? yes, and drinks too.

LAURA.—Will. Burnside——

SUSIE.—Oh, Laura, that's Nettie's devoted admirer; you'd best not discuss him in her presence.

NETTIE.—What a fib, Susie! Go on, Laura.

LAURA.—Will. Burnside takes his social glass. I don't think he uses tobacco in any form.

NETTIE.—Robert Baker and Arthur Wood both drink occasionally, and Morris Hall——

SUSIE.—[*Clapping her hands.*] Oho, Miss Laura! he's *your* beau; and he smokes, because I met him yesterday with a meerschaum in his mouth nearly a yard long. And he loves his wine, too, for I have seen him drink it.

LAURA.—[*Embarrassed.*] Very well; who else? but I think the list is sufficiently long for the present.

SUSIE.—[*Pouting.*] I'd thank you not to slight *my* Fred; he's the best-looking man of the whole lot.

NETTIE.—Really you must pardon the omission, Susie; it was unintentional. Fred. Allen smokes, chews, drinks.

LAURA.—These young men are, without exception, talented, educated, and move in the highest circle of society; several are professors of religion, and yet all are addicted to habits which, unless abandoned, will make slaves of them. The use of tobacco injures and debases a man physically, mentally, and morally, and I am sustained in this assertion by the most eminent and learned physicians.

NETTIE.—Why, Laura, what has induced you to think and speak so earnestly in regard to this subject?

LAURA.—I will tell you. On New Year's, a majority of the young men whose names have been mentioned, made the usual calls during the day. Some were chewing gum or anise-seed to disguise the odor of the cigars which were only laid aside at the door. Some paid two or three visits to the spittoon during a brief call of ten minutes; and, worse than all, the mingled fumes of the different liquors which many of them had imbibed at the houses of the numerous friends whom they had visited, seemed more strongly suggestive of a bar-room than a lady's parlor. Not one of them, I suppose, has ever been intoxicated, or has caused his friends any anxiety by this very moderate, temperate use of spirituous liquors; but I contend that they are all in imminent danger, for this insidious appetite will increase and become more and more powerful, until its victims are drawn down into a vortex of degradation and shame, bringing ruin upon themselves, and sorrow and misery to kindred and friends.

SUSIE.—Nonsense, Laura! you have suddenly turned preacher, and are trying to make out innocent things to be great sins as black as crows. Some of the very nicest, handsomest young men I know—real *tip-top* fellows—smoke and chew, and sometimes take a glass of something to drink; and I don't see that it harms them. Of course they know when to stop. I wouldn't give a straw for a man who hasn't a will of his own; it's only weak-minded, soft-pated men who get drunk.

NETTIE.—Laura, I am truly glad you have introduced this important subject; I heartily coincide with every sentiment you have uttered, and will join you in any plan you may suggest, that will enable us to do what little we can towards eradicating the evils we have been discussing —especially this moderate drinking.

SUSIE.—For shame, Nattie! you have left *me* the alternative of retreating ignominiously, unless I should be brave enough to maintain the field against you both, and then I'm afraid I should be ingloriously defeated; I think I'll neither run nor surrender just yet, however. As to the assertion, that the use of tobacco is injurious, I'll not attempt to refute that at present, for I am such an ignorant little goosie, I should only make sport for you two learned ladies. But what is there so extremely filthy and disagreeable about it? Some people rather like the smell of a good cigar; as for myself, I never spent a thought on the subject.

LAURA.—How often do you walk down the street without being half blinded and choked by the clouds of smoke that float back from almost every passing masculine? and does not every smoker carry about with him a stale, sickening, intolerable odor that pervades his clothes, his breath, and even his whiskers and hair? As for chewing, I repeat that it *is* a filthy, disgusting habit. You know well enough that you cannot go a block without having to gather up your skirts and hop over the streams and puddles of tobacco juice deposited there by these "tip-top" lords of creation. In public halls, in street cars, and even on the steps and in the vestibules of churches, the same nuisance abounds, for no place is too sacred to escape its unclean presence. To put the question right home—what man would live with a wife who, when greeting him fondly on his daily return home, would put up her mouth to be kissed, with the stains of tobacco juice on her lips and a quid tucked away in her cheek? or who would sit on his knee and puff away at a strong cigar or monstrous meerschaum? Would he not turn from her with unspeakable disgust? and yet women are compelled to submit to these abominable, loathsome things without murmuring.

SUSIE.—You've extinguished me entirely, Laura; I must admit that tobacco is *not* such a nice thing, after all. But now about the harmless glass that some of our young friends take now and then. I am confident not one of them would ever be seen at the bar of a restaurant or drinking saloon. Only drunkards, and those who are becoming so, will be found at such places—men who have lost all self-respect.

LAURA.—But what sends the drunkards to these places, especially those whom you denominate as just "*becoming* drunkards?" Is not the appetite formed by the "harmless glass" that they speak of so lightly, that is passed round at social parties, receptions, and weddings, until the desire for strong drink increases, and they then resort to restaurants and saloons?

NETTIE.—Really, Laura, I view this subject in a different light altogether. You have given me some ideas that I shall not soon forget. But what is to be done? what *can* be done?

SUSIE.—That's the question. I admit all that Laura has said, but what *is* the use of groaning about a state of affairs that can't be changed? "what *is* to be, *will* be;" that's my belief, so let's stop this long talk and go out for a walk.

NETTIE.—Not yet, Susie. I think Laura may suggest a plan by which we can accomplish something.

SUSIE.—Oh, you stupid, tiresome old fogies! well I suppose I must be resigned. [*Puts on a comical air of resignation.*]

LAURA.—Yes, we *can* accomplish something. It is

part of woman's mission to refine the minds and elevate and improve the morals of men. We have a broad field before us; let us begin from this day to exert an influence upon our male friends which will result in their attaining to a higher standard of moral excellence. Let us tell them that true manliness will not be fettered by the chains of unhallowed appetite, but will struggle against temptation, and rise above all habits and practices inconsistent with manly dignity and genuine nobility of character.

SUSIE.—You surely don't mean that we are to resolve ourselves into a Total Abstinence and Anti-Tobacco Society, for the purpose of delivering lectures to all the good-looking young men we know, whenever an opportunity offers, do you?

NETTIE.—[*With animation.*] Yes, that's the very idea! I fully agree with Laura, that it is incumbent upon us to exert our influence in behalf of the moral reformation of those around us; to speak warning words to those who are thoughtlessly dallying with temptation, seemingly unconscious of the dangers before them.

LAURA.—I'm glad, Nettie, to have gained so valuable an ally. Perhaps you and Susie will term me a radical, when I here announce my firm determination to accept neither the general nor special attentions of any gentleman who, after having the subject fully presented for his consideration, continues to smoke, chew, or drink. If he likes tobacco or liquor more than me, he can have the benefit of the preference.

NETTIE.—Bravo, Laura! that pleases me immensely. I'm with you heart and hand,

SUSIE.—Bah! tell *that* to the marines. You'll both sing a different tune when certain young cavaliers that I know, happen to "pop the question;" and judging by their increasing devotion, that event is not far in the future. Then we'll *see* what your heroic resolutions amount to.

NETTIE.—We say what we mean, and mean what we say. To the question-popping part of your remark, I will only reply that if Fred. Allen does not propose before a week has passed, I shall be much surprised.

SUSIE.—[*Springing up hastily.*] There! Fred. is to call for me at four o'clock to go to the picture gallery. and I had forgotten entirely. I shall not be ready in time, I know. [*Hurries out.*]

LAURA.—What a careless, thoughtless creature! [*A rap.* LAURA *goes to the door and receives a letter. Examines the address and delivers it to* NETTIE.] Something for you, Nettie.

NETTIE.—[*Opens letter; reads a few lines, and seems much agitated.*] Excuse me, Laura; I will retire to my room to read and reply to this communication.

LAURA.—Certainly, Nettie. [N. *retires.*] That was Will. Burnside's writing, and from Nettie's agitation, I should judge it to be a proposal. Her newly-formed resolution will now be tested, for Will. loves the sparkling wine. Suppose *I* should be called to decide this important question, would my courage waver? If ever man loved woman, Morris Hall loves me, though he has never revealed it in words. How generous and kind hearted, how noble and unselfish he is!—and yet he is a moderate drinker, and smokes to excess. [*A rap. She admits* FRED. ALLEN.] Good-day, Mr. Allen; be seated.

ALLEN.—Thank you. Is Miss Susie ready? [*Takes something from his vest pocket and puts it in his mouth.*]

LAURA.—She will be down in a few minutes. Excuse me, Mr. Allen, but I have some curiosity to know what you are chewing.

ALLEN.—Well—you know, Miss Laura—that is—the fact is, we young men indulge in smoking occasionally, and it is deemed polite and desirable to use something which—you understand, Miss Laura—which—

LAURA.—How can I understand unless you explain.

ALLEN.—Well, then, it is desirable to use something

to disguise the odor that a cigar unavoidably leaves on the breath. But, really, as ladies are not supposed to take an interest in such things, you embarrassed me somewhat. I have in my mouth at present some aromatic seed; the name I do not remember.

LAURA.—Why render the necessary to deodorize the breath before going into ladies' society? Is smoking essential to health or happiness, and does it——

SUSIE.—[*Appears attired for the street, drawing on her gloves.*] How do you do, Fred.? Sorry I've kept you waiting; Laura and Nettie have been discussing tobacco and moderate drinking, and in listening to their learned disquisitions I almost forgot our engagement for this evening. If you wish to keep in their good graces, never allow another atom of tobacco, or a drop of anything stronger than coffee, to touch your lips. Come, I'm ready.

ALLEN.—[*Rising.*] Miss Laura had just opened her batteries upon me when you entered.

LAURA.—I hope Susie will keep up a constant fire upon the enemy's works; or, to speak seriously, convince you that the use of tobacco and stimulants is unnecessary, undignified, and injurious.

SUSIE.—No, indeed! I can't talk scientifically and philosophically, and all that sort of thing, like you can, consequently the effect of my argument, even if I could produce any, would be lost. Come on Fred. [*As they leave, they are met by* MORRIS HALL, *with whom they all exchange merry greetings.*]

MORRIS.—I am happy to meet you alone, Laura, as important business calls me away to-morrow to be absent a month, and before leaving, I desire to speak to you on a subject which deeply affects my present and future happiness. [*Draws his seat near and takes her hand.*] You cannot be ignorant of the fact, that for months past my feeling towards your have been deeper and warmer than those of friendship, and the encouragement and favour I have received have induced the flattering belief that you do not consider me altogether unworthy of your regard. You know that I am a man of plain speech and few wards. I can only say, dear Laura, I love you! will you be my wife?

LAURA.—[*Much embarrassed.*] Morris, you have taken me by storm; this is a serious subject. I must have time to think.

MORRIS.—Time to think! Do you not sufficiently understand the feelings of your heart to answer me now? We know not what may transpire ere we meet again; do not send me on my journey without the promise of your love to cheer me during my absence.

LAURA.—Morris, I will speak frankly. No other has won so high a place in my regard as yourself, and I will confess that the words you have uttered meet a ready response from my heart; but before I can give you the assurance you desire, certain conditions must be complied with.

MORRIS.—[*Throwing his arm across the back of her seat.*] Name them, dearest; I know you are too good and true, to exact anything unworthy or impossible, and the anticipated reward will lighten the most arduous task.

LAURA.—It is no task, Morris, only a simple act of self-denial. You must, from this hour, abstain entirely from the use of tobacco and all intoxicating drinks.

MORRIS.—[*Drops her hand and starts back.*] Laura, you astonish me! You know that for years I have been accustomed to smoking; and though it has been six months since I began to use wine and other light stimulants, more as a social custom, 'tis true, than because I desired them, yet you have never manifested the slightest disapprobation, but have, on more than one occasion, sipped wine yourself. Why, then, this sudden opposition to these harmless indulgences?

LAURA.—I acknowledge with shame and sorrow that I have but recently awakened to a sense of the duty I owe to God and my fellow-creatures. But I have resolved that my future course shall, as far as possible, atone for the past. I shall exert all my influence to induce the young men with whom I associate, to relinquish all unmanly, demoralizing habits, especially that of indulging the appetite for this social glass, which if continued, inevitably leads to the drunkard's awful fate.

MORRIS.—But there can be no possible danger for *me;* there is not a habit to which I am addicted that I cannot at any time abandon without difficulty. I do not think that I smoke enough to be injurious to myself or unpleasant to others; and as for drinking to excess—that can *never* be, for to me there can be no more disgraceful and disgusting object than a drunken man. A well-balanced mind and a proper degree of self-respect will prevent any man from thus degrading himself.

LAURA.—Excuse my plain speaking, Morris, but the odor of cigar smoke that hovers about you at this moment is *decidedly* disagreeable. I assert, moreover, that the wavering, unsettled mind, the want of self-respect, and the blunting, deadening of the sensibilities invariably *follow* the continued use of alcoholic drinks, and are the *results* of drinking, not the causes. [*Pauses a moment.*] I have firmly resolved that I will marry no man who yields to the tempter, even to the smallest extent; and, more than that, the signature of my future husband must be attached to the Pledge of Total Abstinence.

MORRIS.—Laura, you are surely jesting! I cannot be bound by pledges and promises—they are for drunkards, not sober men; it would be betraying a want of confidence in my own moral firmness, integrity, and stability. Do not make this a test of my love, dear Laura. [*Again takes her hand.*]

LAURA.—[*Sadly, but firmly.*] Then, Morris, you can never be more to me than at present. I have witnessed too much sorrow and suffering caused by the intemperance of men who once drank no more than you do, ever to unite my destiny with that of any but a pledged teetotaler.

MORRIS.—Oh, Laura! how can you thus cruelly blight the happiness of one who loves you so fondly? will you not relent?

LAURA.—Morris, my decision is irrevocable! [*Takes up his hat and rushes out.*] So—"the dream is past." He could not bear the test. Oh, Morris! you have left behind you a sad, aching heart, whose love is yours alone. [*Covers her face with her hands, and sighs.*]

SUSIE.—[*Having returned from her walk.*] I say, Laura, what on earth have you been doing to Morris Hall? He rushed by me as I came in, just as though the Evil One was after him; and though he almost upset me in his mad flight, not one word of apology did he offer. If I didn't know him to be your favorite, I should think you had rejected him.

LAURA.—[*Raising her head.*] No, Susie, *he* has rejected *me*. I was in the balance on one side, his social glass and cigars on the other. His love for them was stronger than for me, consequently I am rejected.

SUSIE.—[*Raising her hands with astonishment.*] Well, Laura Bell! so you have been absolutely reducing your high-flown theory to practice, and have lost the handsomest man (but one) in town. You are decidedly the most unmitigated goosie I ever saw! Well, "what is to be, will be," I suppose. But, Laura, I'll tell you a little secret that will help to cheer up your spirits. Fred. and I are engaged—actually *engaged*, and the day appointed. Isn't that nice?

LAURA.—And did you say anything to him on this important subject, Susie?

SUSIE.—Not I. I was so fluttered and agitated, I forgot it entirely; and I'm glad I did, for Fred. might have run off in a crazy way like Morris Hall, and then I should be in the same sad, forlorn condition in which I find poor you. Not exactly though. I should have run

after him and told him he might keep all his pet habits—
that I was only joking; and I expect you wish *you* had
done so, don't you Laura?

LAURA.—No. I do not regret what I have done. If
he loves his " pet habits," as you call them, more than he
loves me, he is not worthy of me.

SUSIE.—Well, I believe Fred. would do anything or
give up anything I should request of him. He'll make a
model husband. [*Goes out singing, and* NETTIE *enters
with an open letter in her hand.*]

NETTIE.—I presume, Laura, you know from whence this
letter came?

LAURA.—I do. And from your agitation, I conjec-
tured its contents.

NETTIE.—I confess candidly, Laura, that it contains a
manly declaration of love and offer of marriage. You are
aware that Will. Burnside has been my constant attendant
for thee years, and during that time I have never known
him to commit a mean or dishonorable act. Had this
arrived one day earlier, I should have returned to him
the unhesitating acceptance my heart would have so
earnestly dictated. But our conversation this morning
has materially changed my views in regard to certain
things, and in my reply, which I dispatched some time
ago, I acquainted him with the convictions of duty lately
aroused in my mind, and stated my determination to marry
no man addicted to the use of strong drink, as I should
constantly be haunted with the fear of becoming that
most wretched of beings—a drunkard's wife. I am sure,
Laura, that you commend my decision.

LAURA.—I do, most heartily. It is the only safe
course. During your absence, I have had an interview
with Morris Hall, who, being compelled to leave town to-
morrow, desires an answer to a certain important question.
My reply was, in substance, the same as yours to Mr.
Burnside; and though I reasoned with him long and
earnestly, his pride could not tolerate the idea of being

bound by pledge ; finally, he left in anger ; and though I would not reverse my decision, still I feel very sad, for Morris has won a place in my heart which no other can ever fill.

NETTIE.—Accept my sincere sympathy, dear friend, and let me cheer you with the thought that a little reflection on his part will bring him to your side again. And now a word in reference to our conversation of this morning. If we entend to carry out our proposed plan, we must have a book prepared for the signatures of all gentlemen whom we can impress with the importance of this course.

LAURA.—I think I have one that will suit our purpose admirably. [*Exit.*]

BURNSIDE.—[*Enters with eager haste, advances to* NETTIE, *who is still standing, and clasps her hands lovingly.*] Darling Nettie, I have just received your note, and could not resist the impulse to come to you immediately. Did you dream for an instant that I would let any foolish habit interpose and obstacle between me and your precious self? No, dearest ; I will gladly submit to your very reasonable requirements, and the more willingly, because I have myself been in serious doubt as to the safety of this social drinking custom. It only needed your sweet, womanly argument to establish my convictions firmly. [*Laura enters unobserved.*] And now this little hand is mine. [*Kisses it.*]

LAURA.—Ahem ! [*Coughs.*]

BURNSIDE.—[*Starting.*] Why, Miss Laura, you entered so much as a spirit, that your suddenly revealed presence startled me.

LAURA.—[*Roguishly.*] Spirits don't wear high-heeled gaiters, and cough to attract the attention of mortals, Mr. Burnside. Nettie, I find that the book I referred to has been used for another purpose, and we have no other that will answer.

BURNSIDE.—There is a bookstore at the corner, ladies ; I shall be happy to supply any want.

LAURA.—We accept your offer with thanks, and delegate you to procure for us a small blank book, in which we propose to write a Pledge.

BURNSIDE.—I will return in a few moments. [*Exit.*]

NETTIE.—And I will get the pen and ink. [*Exit.*]

LAURA.—[*Seating herself in an attitude of sadness and despondency.*] Nettie is happy; and I must *appear* so, even though my heart should break in the sad struggle. [*Covers her face with her hands, and sighs.*]

MORRIS.—[*Appears at the open door—pauses a moment—advances quickly, and dropping on one knee at her side, gently removes her hands.*] Dear Laura, you have conquered! Forgive the foolish pride that for a time obscured my sense and judgment and made me oblivious to my own danger and heedless of your sweet warning. Since our interview, I have calmly weighed every argument you advanced, and I thank you earnestly for the frankness with which you placed the subject before me, and the courage and firmness with which you combated my weak reasoning and refused any compromise with this evil. If all young ladies would pursue the same course, there would be fewer drunkards, and consequently less unhappiness and misery. Will you forgive me and be my own Laura?

LAURA.—All is forgiven, Morris; and I confess that my heart feels much lighter than it did a few moments ago; but I hear footsteps. Oh, Morris, *do* get up. If that wild Susie Gray should catch you in this attitude, we should not escape from her saucy tongue for a month.

MORRIS.—I don't care for Susie or any one else just now—I'm too happy; but to spare your blushes, I will assume a more dignified position. [*Snatches a kiss and springs up, just as* NETTIE *enters at one door and* BURNSIDE *at the other. The three exchange greetings.*]

BURNSIDE.—I have obtained the desired article. [*Hands it to* LAURA.]

LAURA.—Thank you. Now for the Pledge. [*Writes.*]

MORRIS.—What a moral revolution would be produced in society if other ladies would adopt and maintain the principles you two so firmly advocate?

NETTIE.—There is no earthly reason why it should not be so. I am amazed and ashamed that I have lived so long in ignorance of my duty in this respect.

LAURA.—Attention. [*Reads.*] "I solemnly pledge my sacred honor as a man, that I will abstain from all spirituous and malt liquors, wine, and cider as a beverage, and from the use of tobacco in every form. This Pledge to be binding for life." [*Places the book open on the table.*] This is now ready for signatures. [FRED. *and* SUSIE *enter quietly.*]

MORRIS.—I am proud to affix my signature to the Life Pledge. [*Signs.*]

BURNSIDE.—And I will gladly imitate your example. [*Signs.*]

SUSIE.—What wonderful progress! two converts in one day.

NETTIE.—Will you not be the third, Mr. Allen?

ALLEN.—Not at present. It will be time enough when I feel that I need the restraining influence of the Pledge.

BURNSIDE.—I assert positively that you need it fully as much as we do. Miss Susie, *your* persuasive eloquence might move him.

SUSIE.—I believe Fred. has enough pride and common sense to keep him from indulging too freely. When I see him in danger, then I'll use my "persuasive eloquence," as you are pleased to term it. I think this signing the Pledge places one in an awkward position sometimes. Suppose you total abstainers should have a wedding—now don't blush, gentlemen, I'm only supposing the case—would you give your friends nothing but dry cake to eat? for of course wine would be out of the question.

MORRIS.—No. We'd both have some of the nicest lemonade in town, wouldn't we, Will.? [SUSIE *and* FRED. *laugh heartily.*]

SUSIE.—Lemonade with wedding-cake! what a funny idea! But to speak seriously, the Bible recommends wine, though I don't recollect the exact words. Refresh my memory, some of you.

LAURA.—Who hath sorrow? who hath contentions? who hath wounds without cause? They that tarry long at the wine; they that seek strong drink!

BURNSIDE.—Wine is a mocker, strong drink is raging, and whosoever is deceived thereby is not wise!

NETTIE.—Be not among winebibbers, for the drunkard shall come to poverty!

MORRIS.—Look not upon the wine when it is red, when it giveth its color in the cup, for at last it biteth like a serpent and stingeth like an adder!

[*The four in concert.*]—No drunkard shall enter the kingdom of heaven! [SUSIE *and* FRED. *elevate their eyebrows, and raise their hands as if overwhelmed by the texts that follow each other in quick succession, and are uttered with great impressiveness and solemnity.*]

[*Curtain falls.*]

SCENE II.

LAURA *and* NETTIE; *the former turning over the leaves of the Pledge-book.*

LAURA.—As six months have elapsed since the inauguration of our total abstinence movement, I thought I would look over our little book, and I find it contains fifty-eight names. We have been far more successful than I anticipated.

NETTIE.—Many of those whom we induced with great difficulty to sign the Pledge were swiftly going to ruin, but are now sober and prosperous. I am thankful we have been permitted to accomplish so much. [HALL *and* BURNSIDE *enter, exchange customary greetings with the girls, and take seats.*]

MORRIS.—I see you have the Pledge-book, Laura; I often think that had Fred. Allen's name been inscribed in it, he might not have fallen. His boasted pride and self-respect have not restrained his terrible appetite for liquor, for he is now a common drunkard. I met his wife yesterday, and could scarcely recognize her as the saucy, light-hearted Susie who, six months ago, laughed at what she called our "old-fogy notions." She has changed sadly, and I have heard that Fred. is very violent and brutal when intoxicated.

SUSIE.—[*Enters, plainly attired, and in a state of great agitation.*] Dear Laura, will you kindly give your miserable friend shelter for one night?

LAURA.—Certainly, Susie, for as long a time as you wish to stay. [*Leads her to a seat and stands by her.*] May I enquire the cause of your trouble? You appear to be unhappy.

SUSIE.—You are all old and true friends, and have, doubtless, heard of the sad life I have led since my marriage, so I will speak freely. I had not been married a week before I ascertained that my husband had, for a long time, been drinking much more freely than I or any of his friends had imagined; in fact, he acknowledged that he often drank in restaurants and saloons, side by side with the most degraded drunkards. For two months past he has scarcely been sober a day. His business is totally neglected, his money squandered among vile associates. The constant and excessive use of liquor has transformed him into a fiend whose brutal cruelty I can no longer endure. If you will permit me to remain here to-night, I will to-morrow return to my parents, who live in the country, about forty miles from this place. I left them, a happy, merry bride; I shall return, a broken-hearted, wretched woman! [*Heavy footsteps are heard approaching, and a loud, angry voice exclaims,* "Where is she?" SUSIE *crouches in terror behind* LAURA.]

ALLEN.—[*Throws open the door violently. His face*

2

very red ; eyes glaring with rage ; clothing torn and soiled.]
Where is my wife? Ah, you need not try to hide, madam
—I have found you. [*Rushes to her and grasps her arm.*]
Come, march home immediately.

BURNSIDE.—[*Grasping him by the shoulder.*] Allen,
you shall not use any violence toward your wife in our
presence. She desires to remain with Miss Bell to-night,
and I would advise you to leave the room quietly, or you
may compel us to use force.

ALLEN.—She shall not stay here! home's the place
for a married woman, and she *shall* go.

MORRIS.—[*Who has risen.*] The home that *should* be
her dearest refuge, *you* have converted into such a place
of torment that she has been compelled to flee from it.
Fied. Allen, has your manhood utterly forsaken you? Let
your poor, persecuted wife stay where she can find rest
and peace, and go away quietly.

ALLEN.—Seems to me, you're interfering in what don't
concern you.   Did'nt that woman know when she married
me that I took my glass whenever I wanted it? Don't
you remember how she laughed at you for signing the
Pledge, saying at the same time that *I didn't need it?* A
little persuasion from her *then*, would have changed my
wild course and made me a different man, for I would
have sacrificed anything to please her; but she didn't
think it was necessary, aud she's got no right to complain
now.

SUSIE.—He speaks the truth! I know now, when too
late, that my own thoughtless conduct has brought this
grief upon me. When I could easily have turned him
from the path of danger, I laughed at the idea, and refused to exert my influence to win him to a better life.
I have carved my own destiny—and hereafter I will submit to my sad lot without murmuring.

ALLEN.—Now, that's more sensible. What's the use of
fretting about what you can't help, especially as you've
acknowledged that you brought it on yourself.

MORRIS.—Allen, reform—sign the Pledge and be a man again.

ALLEN.—No, sir! I can't do it. Rum and the devil have got such a strong grasp on me, that if I should try to reform, they'd pull me back again. It's no use, I tell you; as long as whiskey's made, and men licensed to sell it, there'll be plenty of drunkards. [*To his wife.*] Come along, Susan. [*Takes a bottle from his pocket and goes out drinking.*]

SUSIE.—Laura—Nettie—I hear that you are both to stand before the altar to-morrow night. May God grant you a happier lot than mine! [*Goes out slowly, weeping.*]

NETTIE.—Poor Susie! hers is indeed a sad fate.

MORRIS.—I am rejoiced to know that on the occasion of the *double bridal*, which will to-morrow night crown our fond hopes with blissful reality, there will be no sparkling ruby wine to tempt our friends to ruin and death.

BURNSIDE.—But as we go through life with our chosen partners beside us—[*each clasps the waist and hand of his intended*]—we will warn the tempted, raise the fallen, and brighten the homes made desolate by the Demon of Intemperance.

LAURA.—And we will still keep our Pledge-book open, and continue to labor for the cause of Total Abstinence.

NETTIE.—And we shall never forget to warn our lady friends, solemnly and earnestly——

L. and N.—*To marry no man if he drinks!*

[*Curtain falls.*]

......

STARTING IN LIFE.

——

Characters.

MRS. MORDAUNT.   THEODORE.

MRS. MORDAUNT *sewing*.

MRS. MORDAUNT.—It is almost time that Theodore was home from school. His last day! Next week he must start into a man's life, leaving behind him these school-boy days that he has found so pleasant. Ah, I hear his step!

Enter THEODORE.

THEODORE.—Well, mother, here I am. My school-days are over at last!

MRS. MORDAUNT.—You have had a pleasant day, I hope?

THEODORE.—Yes, the teachers were all very kind, and gave me their best wishes for success in business-life.

MRS. MORDAUNT.—Are you going out again?

THEODORE.—There is no temptation to go out. The rain pours down in perfect torrents. We have a full hour before dinner-time. Talk to me!

MRS. MORDAUNT.—Imperative case, present tense!

THEODORE.—(*Bowing*.) Will you graciously condescend to converse with your obedient servant?

MRS. MORDAUNT.—Willingly. What shall we talk about?

THEODORE.—About myself. Modest, am I not? But I would like to have a little talk about the future, and you were always my father-confessor, you know!

MRS. MORDAUNT.—Mother-confessor, you mean.

THEODORE.—Many a cat-killing, orchard-robbing, sign-destroying expedition has lost one of its members, by the thought of your gentle reproof, or sorrowful eyes, overpowering his love of mischief at the last moment before starting.

MRS. MORDAUNT.—It makes me very happy to hear you say that, my dear boy. Yet you are almost too old for a lecture, since you look over my head now, with perfect ease.

THEODORE.—Well, good advice need not be a lecture.

MRS. MORDAUNT.—I must confess there are some points where there is room for improvement in your course of conduct.

THEODORE.—I know that well. Take the little sins first, mother, and then attack the big ones.

MRS. MORDAUNT.—The first little sin, then, is the utter waste of your powers of conversation. You are a boy with more than the average amount of brains, of some talent, and have received a good education, and among your gentlemen friends you may use your advantages—of that I cannot judge—but among your lady friends, you are only one degree removed from an empty-headed coxcomb.

THEODORE.—Mother!

MRS. MORDAUNT.—It is an undeniable fact. Once among ladies, you talk the most arrant nonsense, by the hour together.

THEODORE.—Oh mother, not always! I do talk sense sometimes, I am sure.

MRS. MORDAUNT.—When? Recall your conversation last evening in a roomful of clever, sensible girls, and repeat, if you can, one single sentence that you would care to have quoted as a specimen of your conversational powers. Was it not from beginning to end, the smallest of all small talk? The merest twaddle, about weather, opera, and dress, not even rising to the current topics of the day? Come, now, Theodore, be candid.

THEODORE.—But, mother, I don't want the girls to set me down for a pedantic, conceited fellow, anxious to display his own learning. Girls like small talk!

MRS. MORDAUNT.—Do they? Pray upon what foundation do you form that opinion?

THEODORE.—They never talk of anything else but weather, opera, and such subjects.

MRS. MORDAUNT.—Do you ever give them a chance? Did you ever try to lead any of your young lady friends into a sensible, rational conversation, upon some topic that might interest both of you?

THEODORE.—I confess I never did. I thought they liked small talk and flattery.

MRS. MORDAUNT.—Nonsense! If you will confine your remarks entirely to the regions of nonsense, of course the young ladies can do nothing but follow your lead. Do you talk so among gentlemen?

THEODORE.—No; not when we really converse.

MRS. MORDAUNT.—Yet if you were really conversing upon subjects of interest and importance, science, art, politics or literature, what would you do if a party of young ladies entered the room?

THEODORE.—We should all do the same thing.

MRS. MORDAUNT.—And that would first be, to look as guilty as if you were plotting a murder, or as silly as if you had been reading Mother Goose, and then each one of you would turn to your favorite companion among the invaders, compliment her dress and appearance, and set in motion a perfect tide of empty words and phrases.

THEODORE.—I am afraid I must plead guilty!

MRS. MORDAUNT.—Very complimentary to our sex, is it not?

THEODORE.—Having displayed the fault, now for the advice.

MRS. MORDAUNT.—The advice is that the next time you converse with a young lady, you try to confine your conversation within the regions of common sense and

interest, and see if she will not follow you as readily as
into the flowery paths of flattery and compliment.

THEODORE.—I'll try it!

MRS. MORDAUNT.—Next, Theodore, I would cease to
make a chimney of my mouth.

THEODORE.—Oh, mother, a cigar now and then will
not hurt any one!

MRS. MORDAUNT. —I am not so sure of that; and
besides, who can be sure it will be only a *cigar* now and
then?

THEODORE.—I do not chew tobacco.

MRS. MORDAUNT.—I hope not. I should be sorry to
see a son of mine indulging in so disgusting a habit.
Chewing tobacco is not only poisonous to the constitution,
but it is an ungentlemanly, filthy habit, that is offensive
to every person of refinement.

THEODORE.—I quite agree with you.

MRS. MORDAUNT.—Smoking is not much better, even
if indulged in but *moderately*, and who can say moderation in any vice will not lead to excess. Remember the
love for tobacco increases with the indulgence in its use.

THEODORE.—I think two cigars a week will cover all
the indulgence I allow myself in that way. That will not
harm any one.

MRS. MORDAUNT.—Perhaps not. But remember great
vices take root in little faults. Two cigars a week may
lead to four next week, then one each day, two, three, till
what was but a scarcely indulged luxurious taste, becomes
a positive necessity; you will never feel contented unless
you have a cigar between your lips. Then will follow in-
dolence, a torpid drowsiness, and the want of stimulus may
lead you into a love for drink.

THEODORE.—I never craved *that*, mother. It is but
rarely I touch even a glass of wine.

MRS. MORDAUNT.—Like the occasional cigar, Theodore, the wine now and then is a dangerous beginning.

THEODORE.—You advise, then, total abstinence from
liquor and tobacco. ?

MRS. MORDAUNT.—It is the only real safeguard. You can never be certain of yourself, if you once permit the love for either to grow upon you. Now, it is easy to give them up, a year from now, the cessation may entail positive suffering, later may be almost impossible.

THEODORE.—I will consider your words, mother.

MRS. MORDAUNT.—If there were no moral objection, Theodore, drinking and smoking are such vulgar vices. I would have my son a *gentleman*.

THEODORE.—What is a gentleman?

MRS. MORDAUNT.—Are you in earnest?

THEODORE.—Yes. Opinions are so divided. Some of my friends will not wear a coat of last year's cut, because they are afraid of being mistaken for ungentlemanly fellows, yet have no objection to running in debt, and shirking payment for the same. Now can swindling be gentlemanly? Debt contracted without any prospect of payment looks to me like cheating. One man will not swear because it is ungentlemanly, while another will tell you of an oath that it is such a gentlemanly way of swearing; the term seems to me to involve a perfect maze of contradictions, so I ask you again, what is a gentleman?

MRS. MORDAUNT. Pass me the dictionary from the table.

THEODORE.—Now you are laughing at me?

MRS. MORDAUNT.—Not at all. Did you ever look for it in the dictionary?

THEODORE.—Never.

[*Passes dictionary to* MRS. MORDAUNT.

MRS. MORDAUNT.—Here we have a variety of definitions. Sidney pronounces a gentleman "A man of birth; a man of extraction, though not noble."

THEODORE.—That will scarcely answer for our new country.

MRS. MORDAUNT.—Shakespeare informs us that it is "A man raised above the vulgar by his character or post," and again, that "It is used of any man, however high."

THEODORE.—That is better.

MRS. MORDAUNT.—Addison says, "It is a term of complaisance; sometimes ironical."

THEODORE.—It is more than that in this age.

MRS. MORDAUNT.—And Camden says it is: "The servant who waits about the person of a man of rank."

THEODORE.—But none of those definitions will describe a Canadian gentleman of the present day, which I suppose is what you want me to be. Tell me what must *I* do in the arena of my new life, to deserve the title of a true gentleman?

MRS. MORDAUNT.—A true Christian gentleman is the highest moral position a man may attain in this country. First, my son, you must take the golden rule for your constant guide.

THEODORE.—"Do unto others as you would others should do unto you," you mean?

MRS. MORDAUNT.—For unselfishness is the first rule of courtesy. From this spring benevolence and gentleness, and these lay the foundation for the thousand acts of politeness, that in a true gentleman are but the outward symbols of a nobility of soul.

THEODORE.—Christianity, then, is the foundation.

MRS. MORDAUNT.—Undoubtedly. To reach this highest grade of earthly perfection, a thorough Christian gentleman, a man must unite in himself all that is noble and good in the human character. I think it is Ruskin who says, "A gentleman's first characteristic is that firmness of structure in the body, which renders it capable of the most delicate sensation, and of structure in the mind which renders it capable of the most delicate sympathies—one may simply say, fineness of nature."

THEODORE.—But that is reducing the whole to simple refinement.

MRS. MORDAUNT.—Refinement in every sense, moral, physical and mental. How can you go higher? Refined honor can never tolerate a dishonorable action, therefore a refined gentleman must be the soul of honor. Refinement of body will make necessary neatness, and propriety in dress, while it will curb the vulgar display of wealth or extreme fashion.

THEODORE.—Do you class courage among the qualities necessary to form a gentleman?

MRS. MORDAUNT.—True courage, yes.

THEODORE.—You mean moral courage?

MRS. MORDAUNT.—Guiding and directing mere physical bravery. It has been remarked by observers, during many wars, both of late years and in olden times, how far apart were the courage of the gentleman, and that of the ruffian. The latter, displaying mere physical disregard of danger, was made furious by the excitement of battle, and dared everything in a fierce animal love of fighting, and committing injury upon his foes. He threw aside mercy, discipline and self-control, and became a mere sanguinary, revengeful animal, murderer and savage. But the gentleman soldier, fired by the noble enthusiasm of aiding in a good cause, recollecting and fully appreciating his personal danger, accepts the risk, and with his life in his hand, dares as much, and fights as bravely as the most furious ruffian, yet regards discipline, tempers duty with mercy, and keeps his self-command in his most daring onslaught.

THEODORE.—I have often heard people say, they can recognize a *gentleman* as soon as they see one. Can you do so, mother?

MRS. MORDAUNT.—No. I frankly confess that I have been deceived more than once in such decisions. There are many men who have all the polish of manner, all the grace and courtesy of a Chesterfield, yet who are at heart cruel and rude, only deferring to outward observances to shine in society. Others with no knowledge of the etiquette of that society, yet with a heart full of gentle deference to age, weakness or merit, are gentlemen at heart, though they may appear clowns in manner.

THEODORE.—Then it is not well to decide hastily.

MRS. MORDAUNT.—No. Observation of manner is a good test, because a gentleman at heart will have that in his tone and actions that will shine above all the mere surface polish of *mere* society airs.

THEODORE.—It is curious how the authorities vary.

MRS. MORDAUNT.—Some authors define a gentleman as simply one who lives without work.

THEODORE.—But superannuated residents of the alms-house live without work.

MRS. MORDAUNT.—Others define it as one who is able to live in comfort without work, one possessing fortune.

THEODORE.—Mere money cannot make *your* gentleman, mother?

MRS. MORDAUNT.—Never, because I consider idleness as a *vice*. Honorable employment is not derogatory to a gentleman, because it paves the way to independence.

THEODORE.—But if a man already possesses a fortune?

MRS. MORDAUNT.—Then he can find ample employment for his time in works of philanthropy and charity.

THEODORE.—Well, I shall have to make my fortune, before I spend it!

MRS. MORDAUNT.—Another fault against which I would warn you, Theodore, is a tendency to over-dress. What is vulgarly called *flash*-dressing is becoming a vice only too common among our young men. Gay neckties, jewelry in profusion, smart waistcoats, and conspicuous gloves.

THEODORE, *(laughing.)*—A gentleman may not have the scope allowed the fair sex, then?

MRS. MORDAUNT.—No. Custom has decided that quiet colors, and a modest style of dress are more becoming to your sex, so I beg you will not appear again in the very gay waistcoat and necktie with which you dazzled my eyes last evening.

THEODORE.—To hear is to obey.

MRS. MORDAUNT.—Lounging about the streets is another evil. I will not mention whose son it was, I saw last week, leaning against a tree-box, talking to five other boys, apparently as idle as himself.

THEODORE, (*laughing*.)—I am afraid you must own him.

MRS. MORDAUNT.—And that is another of the little sins, against which I would warn you as paths to great vices. Idleness can be cultivated, till it rules soul, mind and body with a rod of iron. Find *something* to do.

THEODORE.—But father told me I might take a month to look about me.

MRS. MORDAUNT.—Look about you, then. Do not waste one day of your month, but gain something in that time that will help you in your future life. And in the train of idleness, you will find wasteful extravagance.

THEODORE.—I know what you mean now. My drive last week, cost me more than I could afford, yet I could not avoid the expense without appearing mean.

MRS. MORDAUNT.—Do not be a slave to the opinions of a set of brainless fellows who want to enjoy themselves at your expense. It is not mean to keep within the limits of your purse. Your character will not stand any higher among sensible people, for wearing clothes more expensive than you can afford; running in debt for suppers you ought not to give; smoking, drinking, gambling, to pass away time you ought to employ in useful labor. You must scorn the ridicule that would lead you to useless extravagance, not fear it.

THEODORE.—Fear is scarcely the word.

MRS. MORDAUNT.—Fear is exactly the word. It is a want of moral courage that leads to half the evils that beset young men, when starting in life.

THEODORE.—There's the sun!

MRS. MORDAUNT.—And you think you have had enough good advice for one day?

THEODORE.—I did not mean that. You have given me subjects for many an hour of thought.

MRS. MORDAUNT.—And prayer, my son. Remember

all my counsels and your good resolutions will be of no avail, unless you ask for strength and guidance from your Heavenly Father. He only can keep your feet in the right path.

THEODORE.—I will remember !

MRS. MORDAUNT.—And now you must go. I am obliged to go out at this hour to take Clara to the dentist's.

[Both go out

AMBITION.

—

Characters.

LAWRENCE.   HENRY.

CHARLES.   FRANK.

PAUL.

*A study. FRANK seated at a table, with an open book before him.
Beside the book upon the table, are pen, paper, ink and a globe.*

FRANK, (*sighing.*)—My head feels fairly dizzy over these
problems, yet I am resolved to conquer them. It will be
a disappointment to my dear father, if I do not take the
prize at this examination, for I resolved to compensate
him for last year's disappointment, by being very studi-
ous. My history, geography, and grammar I have but
little fear about, but mathematics are so hard for me, and
Latin is terrible.

Enter HENRY, PAUL, CHARLES, *and* LAWRENCE.

HENRY.—Come, Frank, we are going up to Turtle Rock
for a boat race, and want you!

FRANK, (*eagerly.*)—A boat race! What boats?

CHARLES.—The Undine and Serpent.

FRANK.—It will be a close match!

LAWRENCE.—Yes, the best regatta of the season. Come,
we are in a hurry!

FRANK, (*rising.*)—I'll be ready in five minutes. No!
[*Resumes his seat.*] I cannot go.

LAWRENCE.—Oh, nonsense! You must go!

FRANK.—I cannot, I have set myself a task to do first.

CHARLES, (*looking at books.*)—Conic sections! Ugh!

LAWRENCE.—Oh, bother conic sections!

FRANK.—I wish I could, for they certainly bother me!

PAUL.—Must you stay, Frank?

FRANK.—Yes, Paul. Father wants me to try for the prize, this year.

LAWRENCE.—You are ambitious, then?

[Laughs sneeringly.

FRANK.—Is that a crime, Larry?

LAWRENCE—That is a very nice question, Frank.

HENRY.—We can spare a little time, and Frank evidently wants a rest from his conic sections. Come, we will have an important debating club. I propose the question. Is ambition a vice or a virtue? *[All take seats.*

LAWRENCE.—Were there no ambitious men, it appears to me that progress must be ended, science would come to a stand-still, and the world stagnate. What truly great man ever left the world a benefactor to his fellow-man, who was not spurred from height to height by ambition?

CHARLES.—Yet an ambitious man in history is considered a vicious man by many writers. We find the quality classed with pride and unscrupulous conduct, while Scripture condemns it, in more than one place.

FRANK.—Ambition led Watt to the highest rounds of the ladder of science.

PAUL.—Ambition caused Satan to be cast from heaven!

LAWRENCE.—Like every quality given to man, ambition may lead him either to perfection or ruin. True ambition appears to me the pure honest desire to excel in whatever we undertake, provided always that we do not suffer our selfish desire to rise, to lead us into doing wrong to our fellow-men, or violating the commands of God. Every lawyer should enter the bar with the aim and hope of becoming a judge; every poet should aspire to being a second Shakespeare; every scientific scholar should hope to discover power as great as steam or magnetism; every soldier should look forward to becoming a general; and every schoolboy should aim at the head of his class, for only that

desire and hope of rising, can make us aim at perfection
in the condition of life we occupy at starting. The man
who is content to plod along in the lowest ranks, will be
found to be indolent, sluggish, and worthless.

PAUL.—Yet Bacon says, "Ambition is like anger
which makes men full of alacrity if it is not checked, but
if it is checked in any manner, and not able to have its
own way, it becomes malign and venomous." Now if
Bacon is right, we can scarcely consider ambition as a
virtue, since it may lead to such disastrous results, and
if not a virtue, it must be a vice.

FRANK.—Yet, without ambition, how much of man's
natural dignity would be lost, since it spurs to exertion all
his highest intellectual powers? Without it, man would
be content to be a poor, debased creature, allowing the
powers of his brain to rust for want of energy to cultivate
and apply them; he could never rise in his profession,
having no *ambition* to reach its highest point. Like
every other good gift it is the abuse and not the use of
ambition's fire, that leads to sin. . Kept within proper
bounds, is a noble quality, leading to perfection.

CHARLES.—But the trouble is, how to limit it! A good
man looks upon content as a virtue; yet an ambitious man
never knows content! However powerful he may be, his
insatiable passion, ambition, spurs him forward to grasp
higher powers, unheeding whom he may overthrow in his
selfish progress, often letting desire usurp the place of
justice, and in the end, dying with an unsatisfied craving
for heights life was not long enough to scale.

LAWRENCE.—No one can deny that the grades of ambition vary with each nature, and that in some the passion
becomes a dangerous and sinful striving for mere wordly
advantage. Yet because ungoverned minds become weak-
ened by their own unlimited desires, it does not follow
that ambition itself becomes a vice. We might as well
say that fire is an evil, because sometimes it destroys, instead of ministering to our own comfort. Ambition is the

strongest incentive to perseverance, and difficulties will sink before it, where they had appeared mountain high. Take, for instance, our great travellers, explorers and discoverers, where could they have gained the energy that led them through heat and cold, exposure and danger, doubt and difficulty, had not ambition kept alive their hope and courage?

PAUL.—Yet inordinate ambition is but the sin of covetousness under another name, for what is coveting, save desiring that which does not belong to us? It leads to avarice, after stimulating to the pursuit of wealth; to tyranny, after power is gained; to disappointment when the glittering bubble we pursue turns to tinsel in our grasp.

FRANK.—Without ambition no great deed was ever accomplished. It is a guiding-star to the wise and good, only a snare to the vain and foolish.

CHARLES.—Ambition caused Napoleon to deluge Europe with blood!

LAWRENCE.—Ambition led Benjamin Franklin to the most wonderful discoveries in Electricity.

PAUL.—Ambition made Richard the Third a murderer.

FRANK.—And Washington a father to his country.

HENRY.—Very well argued on both sides. Frank, have you Lilly's Midas?

FRANK.—Not here,

HENRY.—Then I must trust to memory. He says,

> "Ambition hath but two steps; the lowest
> Blood; the highest envy."

while Crown on the other hand says:

> "Ambition is a spirit in the world,
> That causes all the ebbs and flows of nations,
> Keeps mankind sweet by action; without that,
> The world would be a filthy settled mud."

So we close the debate by deciding that: Ambition ruled by Religion and Reason is a virtue: unchecked and maddened by Vanity and Covetousness it is a vice!

3

CHARLES.—It is time for us to be off now, boys. Frank, are you sure you cannot join us?

FRANK.—I will work hard till I have conquered my appointed task, and then, if it is not too late, will come after you.

LAWRENCE.—Good-bye, then, we will not detain you any longer from your work.

ALL.—Good-bye!   [*All go out, except* FRANK.

FRANK.—I think I may trust my ambition, since its aim now is to gratify my father, and prove myself worthy of the pains he is taking to make me a good scholar. I must go to my room for another slate, and then to work again.   [*Goes out.*

*

THE ILLS OF DRAM-DRINKING.

FOR THREE MALES.

(The Drunkard, TOM, must be dressed rather shabbily, and his nose must be reddened ; JOHN, as a respectable working-man, and LOVE-DROP, with a cigar.)

JOHN.—Well, Tom, how are you ?   I have not seen you for a long time.

TOM.—I am not very well.

JOHN.—What is the matter with you ?

TOM.—Why, I don't exactly know.   I feel very weak and languid, as well as thirsty and miserable.   I suppose I must go and get another pint or two to set me all right.

JOHN.—A pint or two of what ?

TOM.—Of the very best beer.

JOHN.—Can you tell me what your beer is made of ?

TOM.—No.

JOHN.—Water, treacle, poison, and a little putrefied vegetable matter.

TOM.—I don't care; it's the best medicine that ever was invented, for I have tried it before.

JOHN.—How much did you take ?

TOM.—About half a dozen pints, more or less.

JOHN.—That must be a very queer way of taking medicine; six pints in a day !   But please tell me how you felt after this large dose.

TOM.—I felt as if everything was upside down, myself included ; and every now and then the ground would seem to jump up and hit me on the head.   I felt as if I could fight anybody, and was very proud of trying to walk both sides of the path at once.

JOHN.—Your medicine operated very curiously; but did it cure you?

TOM.—Yes, that it did for the time.

JOHN.—But how did you feel the next morning ?

TOM.—This is the next morning, and it was only last

night I tried the experiment, and I have already told you how I feel; but I omitted to tell you that I shall not be able to get my full dose to-day, because I am very light in three places.

JOHN.—Where are they?

TOM.—My stomach, my head, and my pocket.

JOHN.—So, after you have tried your miraculous medicine, you find the effects are, firstly—it removed your malady for the time, only for it to return with increased violence; secondly—it rendered you incapable of governing yourself; in plain terms, you were drunk; thirdly—it created a desire to return again to the so-called medicine; fourthly—it made you light in the three places you have mentioned. Now I want to have a word with you about this drink. You were at one time fond of argument.

TOM.—Well, talk away then, only don't be long over it, for I am as thirsty as a herring.

JOHN.—You don't seem to care much about the matter; but first ask me some question, for I can't knock anything down before it's built up.

TOM.—Did not Solomon say a pint of beer was a good thing for a working-man?

JOHN.—No.

TOM.—Then didn't somebody tell Timothy to take a drop of gin for his stomach's sake?

JOHN.—Not exactly that either; but is there anything the matter with your stomach?

TOM.—It's rather empty, that's all.

JOHN.—Then what do you think is the best thing to fill it with?

TOM.—Why, some beer, to be sure.

JOHN.—Can you tell me what becomes of the beer after you have drank it?

TOM.—It fills up my stomach, and answers the purpose of a good dinner.

JOHN.—How much do you think your stomach is capable of holding?

Tom.—I have read in some books, when I was young, about two pints.

John.—Then what a foolish man you must be, to try and get six pints into a two-pint measure.

Tom.—I never thought of that before.

John.—Do you not see that a pound of bread would usefully fill your stomach, while the injurious beer is immediately absorbed into your system?

Tom.—It's of no use talking to you; you've been better educated than I have; but when I have been to the Half Moon and got primed, I will come back and talk to you. But in the mean time, here is Mr. Lovedrop—he will soon settle you. (*Exit.*)

(*Enter* LOVEDROP.)

Lovedrop.—Well, friend John, how are you?

John.—In the very best of health. How are you?

Lovedrop.—Oh, pretty well, except a light bilious headache; but say, I have heard you are a teetotaler!

John.—I *am* a teetotaler, and I am proud of it.

Lovedrop.—The more fool you to join such a set of enthusiasts; you may as well condemn the whole system of navigation, because some get drowned in the practice of it.

John.—All great men were enthusiasts in the particular branch of science or art that they excelled in; Newton, Hunter, Davy, and others. The proper meaning of the word is " man in earnest." The case you state about navigation does not apply to the subject; drinking intoxicating drinks is not necessary, may be done without altogether, and their use is highly dangerous to the community; while navigation is both necessary and useful!

Lovedrop.—I contend that the little drop I take does me no harm.

John.—Define your term; how much is a little drop?

Lovedrop.—Three glasses in a day.

John.—That would amount to above one thousand glasses a year; rather a large drop.

LOVEDROP.—Did not Christ make wine at the marriage feast in Cana?

JOHN.—Yes; but you cannot prove that it was intoxicating wine; on the contrary, we have evidence to prove that it was not so. I heard a very good answer to that in a meeting once. A little boy was making a speech, and occasionally quoted texts of Scripture, when a crusty old bachelor got up and inquired sneeringly of the boy, if Christ did not make wine at the marriage-feast; the boy replied that he was too young and the gentleman was too old, as well as too ugly, to get married; that if they only drank wine at their marriage-feasts, there would not be much danger of their ever becoming sots.

LOVEDROP.—Did not Noah get drunk?

JOHN.—And do you believe he was any the better for it? on the contrary, he was much the worse, and if a wise and good man like Noah could not withstand the temptation, how much more likely are you to be borne down before it?

LOVEDROP.—There is no danger of my falling into the temptation.

JOHN.—Yes there is, a very great danger; do you know a single drunkard who at one time had the remotest idea of ever becoming what he is?

LOVEDROP.—You are assuming that I associate with drunkards, which is not the case. I drink in moderation, because it helps to support the government, you see.

JOHN.—It must be a poor government which cannot get along without that drink which causes such crime, poverty, and wretchedness as is everywhere visible. Both government and society lose by it in the end, for if the sale of strong drinks were utterly and forever prohibited by law, three-fourths of the jails and work-houses would perish with them.

LOVEDROP.—But what would become of the distillers and saloon proprietors?

JOHN.—What do they deserve to be done with, who sell out that liquid curse which destroys sixty thousand men in a year?

LOVEDROP.—But they are respectable members of society, and must be done something with.

JOHN.—Let them turn farmers and cultivate the ground, and learn to use its products to a better purpose than to make drinks which proves the curse of the country.

LOVEDROP.—The teetotalers don't go the right way to work, trying to get a Maine Law, and prohibit the sale; they ought to try to get individuals to give up, and in time the whole community would become moderate.

JOHN.—Why don't you join us then, and show us a more excellent way, instead of swelling the ranks of the enemy? Your argument would apply with equal force to the law against stealing and other vices.

LOVEDROP.—When I get into company they will have me drink, and besides I like it and it seems to do me good; I can't give it up.

JOHN.—Can't! You ought to be ashamed to say so. I have given it up, and if you can't I am a better man than you. As to the drink seeming to do you good, your bilious headache is a case in point. Half the ills that flesh is heir to may be traced, directly or indirectly, to the use and abuse of stimulants.

LOVEDROP.—Why, my dear sir, you would not certainly deny that liquor does good in some cases?

JOHN.—Very few cases indeed can be cited where it does good. You know that the medical profession is now rapidly discarding its use as a medicinal agent; and as a beverage it is now pronounced hurtful, debilitating and full of misery in the future to every man who imbibes the accursed thirst for ardent spirits.

LOVEDROP.—I will think upon what you have said, but I am afraid it's no use at my time of life.

JOHN.—It's never too late to mend; but I see you are like many other moderates; your judgment says, abstain, but your palate says, I like a little drop.

LOVEDROP.—Well, I can't stop any longer, so good-bye.

JOHN.—Good-bye; but think of what I have told you, and attend our meetings.

CHOOSING A TRADE.

Characters.

MR. MORGAN.	CHARLES.	EDWARD.
ALFRED.	DAVID.	FRANK.
GODFREY.	ISAAC.	MARK.

MR. MORGAN *reading*; CHARLES *reading*; EDWARD *and* ALFRED *playing chess*; DAVID *and* GODFREY *playing backgammon*; ISAAC *and* MARK *writing*.

CHARLES—(*looking up from his book.*)—I should like to be a great author !

MR. MORGAN.—What has inspired you with that desire so suddenly?

CHARLES.—Reading Milton at this moment, Macaulay yesterday, and Dickens perhaps to-morrow. Is it not a great gift, that by the written thought issuing from one man's pen, thousands may be instructed, pleased, perhaps led from vice to virtue, from sin to God?

MR. MORGAN.—It is indeed a noble profession, when taken up in the spirit which you describe, Charles. Not adopted merely for money or fame, but with the sincere desire to ennoble your fellow-men, diffuse knowledge and lead to Christianity. But it is no play to be such an author.

CHARLES.—I know that, sir. But I will study hard to gain knowledge now, that when I take up my pen in future, I may rank as a *great* author.

EDWARD.—And I shall study hard too, Charles, to do for men's bodies what you purpose to do for their minds.

MR. MORGAN.—You will be a doctor, Edward?

EDWARD.—That is my great desire, sir. I would be a famous physician, such as now stand for authorities at the head of their profession.

MR. MORGAN.—You must be a close student, to realize that dream.

EDWARD.—True. I would study Science in her highest branches, and then seek out practical uses for my knowledge. A doctor has a grand work before him.

MR. MORGAN.—The power of alleviating or preventing suffering is certainly one of the noblest gifts given to man. And no man has such power so completely within his grasp as the conscientious, skilful physician.

EDWARD.—I would be no hermit, to shut myself within four walls for the purpose of crowding my own brains with knowledge, but in the hospitals, among the poor, wherever misery could be relieved, pain conquered, disease baffled, there I would make my study, till I had the science at my own command. And then, Charlie, my hands against your pen, in the work of benefiting mankind.

ALFRED.—I will be a sailor!

CHARLES.—You, Al! I thought you were to be Edward's rival in the medical profession?

ALFRED.—So they say at home, but the student's life has no charm for me. I would lead an active life, wrestle with the elements, dare the storm in its fury, court the breeze in its mild humor, till I had steered my vessel safely from port to port, bearing the spices of the East, the furs of the North, the jewels of the South, to trade for our own corn and cotton. Or, upon a man-of-war, do battle for my country's flag, and place my name upon the roll of honor, now blazoned in our navy.

FRANK.—I aspire to becoming an inventor.

MR. MORGAN.—Of what?

FRANK.—Something in the way of a magnetic telegraph, or an iron-clad, sir. [*All laugh.*] I am content to commence in an humble way, and take my position as apprentice in a machine shop. I will learn to file a hammer and bore; will study mechanical drawing, will master civil engineering, until from a workman, I rise to a higher position, master of my trade, knowing the relative powers of material and force, and when my name appears on a patent as important as the locomotive or sewing machine, you fellows will all laugh on the other side of your mouth! Then Charles may write verses to my honor, Alfred may carry my fame abroad——

CHARLES.—And Edward patch up your worn-out brains and body.

DAVID.—I should like to be a lawyer. Law is the lever by which crime is——

CHARLES.—Elevated to the gallows.

DAVID.—You shut up, you've had your say. You have spoiled one of the most eloquent defences of the law, ever spoken outside of a court-room. Perhaps it is just as well, for I can never realize my wish.

MR. MORGAN.—Why not, David?

DAVID.—Father is going to teach me his trade, sir, and expects me to go into his store.

EDWARD.—What is his trade?

DAVID.—Shoemaking!

CHARLES.—"Oh, what a fall was there, my country-men!"

DAVID.—From the judge's wig, to his honor's boots! Well, he shall have good boots if I make them, anyhow.

MR. MORGAN.—That's the right spirit, David. If you are obeying your father, and performing faithfully the duty appointed for you, you will be as happy and useful on the shoemaker's bench as on the judge's.

DAVID.—What shall you be, Godfrey?

GODFREY.—A merchant. I shall charter Alfred's vessel, and many more, to send to every known port, to collect wares for my stores. I shall open paths of employment for hundreds of my fellow-men. Sailors shall man my vessels, clerks fill my counting-houses, salesmen my stores. My wealth shall find a thousand avenues to benefit others, while enriching myself.

MR. MORGAN.—An honest, liberal merchant, may do all this, Godfrey; yet watch carefully, lest the love of amassing wealth contract your philanthropy, till it becomes avarice.

ISAAC.—I will be a traveler. I will explore the burning plains of Africa, and the frozen paths of the Arctic regions, the deserts of the East, the prairies of the West, will cross the trackless ocean, and journey over the land, culling from every clime her hidden treasures of knowledge. My books shall rival those Edward writes, for I will deal only with observation and facts. My pen shall print for others what my eyes find worthy of record, and I will place my name among the great explorers.

CHARLES.—Unless you are eaten up by some of the lions of Africa.

DAVID.—Or the Polar bears.

ALFRED.—Captured by the Arabs.

GODFREY.—Or scalped by the Indians.

ISAAC.—Bah! Every life has its dangers. Why do you not threaten Charles with a brain fever, Edward with the small-pox, Alfred with drowning, and Frank with mutilation?

MR. MORGAN.—Your defence is just, Isaac. Every profession has its dangers, and a coward would shirk all. But what will our quiet little Mark be?

MARK.—A missionary, sir.

MR. MORGAN.—A noble life, Mark.

MARK.—I trust to be allowed to realize my wish, sir. My father is willing for me to study for the ministry. And when I am ready, all my schoolmates may aid me in my work.

CHARLES.—How, Mark ?

MARK.—Isaac shall tell me where in his travels he finds the greatest need of my services.

ISAAC.—I'll hunt up heathens for you, never fear.

MARK.—Godfrey shall lend me a berth in one of his vessels, to carry me to my destination.

GODFREY.—It shall be fitted up like a parlor for you.

MARK.—Alfred shall steer my ship across the ocean.

ALFRED.—That I will, heartily.

MARK.—Frank shall aid me in imparting the mysteries of mechanics to my scholars.

FRANK.—I'll invent machines for their special benefit.

MARK.—Edward shall pack my medicine chest.

CHARLES.—I will write your fame !

DAVID.—And I will make your boots !

MR. MORGAN.—It gives me great pleasure, dear boys, to find that you all seek to benefit others, not attain merely your own selfish ends. The man who makes wealth, or even fame, the sole object for which he works, will arrive at his journey's end with a sordid and hardened heart. But he who, in his daily routine of duty, will watch for the opportunity of aiding others, elevating his fellow-men, and doing good, whether he be poet or merchant, doctor or mechanic, shoemaker or traveller, lawyer or missionary, must become respected and beloved, and carry a clear conscience and happy heart.   [Curtain falls.

THE SCHOOLMASTER ABROAD.

Characters.

JOHN.   HENRY.
THOMAS.   LOUIS.
ARTHUR.   PETER.
      JOE.

The boys all seated at their desks. A number of other boys at desks. JOHN in the teacher's seat.

JOHN, (*striking desk with ruler.*)   Silence !
                              [*In a loud voice.*

THOMAS.—Nobody is making a noise but you.

JOHN.—Silence, I tell you!   [*In a louder voice.*

HENRY.—Set an example, if you want silence.

JOHN.—Silence !   [*As loud as he can speak.*

LOUIS.—Silence !

ALL THE BOYS.—Silence !

JOHN.—Having produced silence from the whole of you, we will now proceed to the day's studies. First class in history ! [*All jump up.*] Keep your seats, but answer the question· [*All sit down.*] Who discovered America ?

HENRY.—Peter the Hermit !

THOMAS.—Queen Victoria !

LOUIS.—Louis Napoleon !

PETER.—Martin Van Buren !

JOE.—Hail Columbia !

JOHN.—Was there ever such a set of blockheads ? Christopher Columbus discovered America—in—in—well, some time ago!

HENRY.—Bully for him!

THOMAS.—Three cheers for Chris! [*All cheer three times.*

JOHN.—Silence! What do you mean by all this racket?

LOUIS.—Give it up!

JOHN.—Louis, you are so smart! Who beheaded Cromwell?

LOUIS.—Oh! oh! oh! [*All the boys echo, oh! oh! oh!*

JOHN.—Stop that noise! Louis, answer the question.

LOUIS.—I can't;

JOHN.—Henry, you answer it!

HENRY.—Never knew before he was beheaded!

JOHN.—I never heard of such gross ignorance! Never knew Charles the first was beheaded?

LOUIS.—You said Cromwell!

JOHN.—It's all the same thing.

HENRY.—I bet Charles didn't think so!

JOHN.—Thomas, who beheaded Charles the first?

THOMAS.—The executioner.

JOHN.—Louis, what are you giggling about?

LOUIS.—I, sir? I was only smiling serenely.

JOHN.—Go to the dunce stool.

LOUIS.—Certainly, sir. [*Goes and sits on dunce stool.*

JOHN.—Henry!

HENRY.—Here, sir.

JOHN.—Hold your tongue, and tell me who was the first President of the United States.

HENRY.—How can I tell you, if I hold my tongue?

JOHN.—Hold your tongue, sir, and answer me!

HENRY.—(*holding his tongue with his fingers.*) John Jacob Astor.

JOHN.—Who? Speak distinctly.

HENRY, (*letting his tongue go.*)—Louis the Fourteenth!

JOHN.—I am ashamed of you. Who was the father of his country?

HENRY.—The son of its grandfather, sir.

JOHN.—No levity, sir!

HENRY.—The husband of its mother, then.

JOHN.—Go sit on the dunce stool, you blockhead!

[HENRY *sits in* LOUIS' *lap.*

JOHN.—Thomas, do you know your geography lesson?

THOMAS.—You'll find out, when you hear it.

JOHN.—Bound Maine.

THOMAS.—Can't do it, sir. The boundless main is proverbial.

JOHN.—Where are the Andes?

THOMAS.—All my aunties are at home, thank you, sir.

JOHN.—How long is the Amazon River?

THOMAS.—Just three inches, sir, on my map. It is rather longer on the map against the wall.

JOHN, (*sternly.*)—I'll have no more nonsense! Where is Georgia?

THOMAS.—Down South, and no nonsense about it!

JOHN.—Go to the dunce stool, sir.

[THOMAS, *goes and sits on* HENRY'S *lap.*

JOHN.—Arthur, what is a conic section?

ARTHUR.—The most comic section I was ever in, sir, was the negro minstrel's hall.

JOHN.—Conic, Arthur!

ARTHUR.—Yes sir: comic Arthur, if you will!

JOHN.—Arthur, if ten tons of grain cost one hundred dollars, how many cattle will it feed?

ARTHUR.—I don't believe the cat'll eat ten tons, sir. Our cat won't anyhow.

JOHN.—Arthur, you are too smart for this school. I shall be obliged to dismiss you.

ARTHUR.—Thank you! [*Jumps up.*

JOHN.—But first, you may sit an hour on the dunce stool. ARTHUR *sits on* THOMAS' *lap.*

JOHN.—Peter, do you know your definitions?

PETER.—I don't know, sir.

JOHN.—Don't know what, your definitions?

PETER.—I don't know if I know my definitions or not.

JOHN.—Define Cosmopolitan.

PETER.—Cricky!

JOHN.—Not the proper definition. Go to the dunce stool.   [PETER *sits in* ARTHUR'S *lap.*

LOUIS.—I say, John, it's getting rather heavy here. Some of you fellows come underneath.

          [*Slips out, and they all fall down.*

JOHN.—Order there!

HENRY.—You undertook to order for all of us.

JOHN.—Sit down, all of you!

[*All try for the stool, finally sit as before,* LOUIS *on* PETER'S *lap,* HENRY *on the stool.*]

JOHN.—Joseph!

JOE.—(*in a squeaking voice.*) That's me! Short for Joe!

JOHN.—Joseph, what is a verb?

JOE.—Part of speech, sir.

JOHN—Very good! What part!

JOE.—The—the—verbal part!

JOHN.—Oh Joe! Joe! What a dunce you are!

HENRY.—Oh John! John! here comes the teacher!

    [*All hurry to their seats, and begin to study out loud.*

                    [*Curtain falls.*

....

MODERATION;

OR I CAN TAKE IT OR LEAVE IT ALONE.

———

BY THOMAS RITCHIE.

I became acquainted with Mr. A., in a neighboring city, some considerable time ago, and formed a great liking to him. He was intelligent, frank, and lively; in a word, essentially a social being. Just one of the class who stand on dangerous ground, though having an instinctive dislike to excess or coarse debauchery. Though then a drinking man myself, I was older than he, and had seen enough of the evils of intemperance and the deceitfulness of strong drink, to make me wish to put him on his guard; but the opportunity never presented itself until about a year afterwards, when I was so situated that I could enforce precept with example.

Mr. A. had arrived in our village, on business; and immediately after his arrival I met him at a corner of a street. After the usual salutations, the following conversation ensued:

Mr. A:—Is there no decent place here where we can get a drop of something to clear the cob-webs from our throats; I feel deucedly husky this morning.

B.—Since I saw you last I have come to think that no rum shop can be a decent place; and, I am sorry to say, that those of our village are of almost the lowest order.

Mr. A.—What, B! Sworn off. No more jolly times, no more of the spirited toasts, no more sallies of wit, under the influence of the "rosy." I am astonished at you!

B.—Not more so than I am at myself. I am astonished that, knowing the insinuating nature of social habits, and

4

the dreadful effects of confirmed drunkenness, to which all social drinking tends, I did not, long ago, renounce the cursed habit of tippling.

Mr. A.—Well, I will, of course, allow that confirmed drunkenness is bad, and brings much misery into the world; but you pay a poor compliment to yourself, if you say you were in danger of becoming a slave to drink, as all drunkards must be. I think you had strength of mind enough to guard against that, and I, for one, can take a glass or let it alone. I dare say if I thought I were in danger of becoming a drunkard I should do as you have done. Besides, I must say I like a glass now and then, especially when the company is good.

B.—Well, the ice is broken, and I will speak plainly to you. Now, or perhaps never, is your time to escape the danger. You own you like a glass, and I know you like good company, which in your estimation consists of social merry fellows, and from these likings almost entirely grow intemperance and drunkenness, among refined and sensitive natures. Apart from this easy entrance into the Domains of Bacchus, no man, with a nature such as I give you credit for, would ever find himself associating with the bully, the *loafer*, to use an Americanism, and the thief. Yet, such cases are altogether too common: And you may become another sad exemplification of it.

Mr. A.—Nonsense. If I were to find the habit getting the better of me, I should stop at once; but, as I said before, I can take it or leave it alone.

B.—I do not doubt that you can now; but what guarantee have you that you will always be able to make this boast. You know the old saying, "Habit is second nature." According to my observation, habit, at least the habit of drunkenness is stronger than nature, for it will make a high-souled, honorable man, the meanest thing that crawls; it will lead him to borrow money without the least idea of paying it, and to beg for liquor, from people that formerly he would have been ashamed to be seen with. A man does not become a drunkard all at once;

there would be few were such the case. The change
would appal the most abandoned. But the steady use of
liquors affects the nerves and weakens the will; and by the
time the poor moderate drinker sees the evils of intemperance in his own case, ten chances to one he has not force of
will to make an effort for freedom: Alcohol, in some
shape, is almost necessary to his existence.

Mr. A.—Why B., you talk like an oracle, but I must
say, I think your new-found zeal carries you too far, and
to some extent, warps your judgment. But, as I said before,
I am husky, and if you will not accompany me I must take
a nip alone, for I think I see the picture of a Lion with a
suspiciously blue nose round the corner, and I shall test
his hospitality.

B.—Hold on, A. I don't like to think of your drinking
alone; and, as I cannot accompany you, let me introduce you
to Mr. C., an acquaintance of mine, who, I daresay, will be
glad to show you the mysteries of the Blue Lion bar-
room.

Mr. A. looked suspiciously at me, for Mr. C., who
had just arrived on the ground, and to whom I introduced
him, showed no indications of belonging to the "Upper
Crust," being unwashed, uncombed, and altogether seedy
in attire. As they left, I told A. I wished to see him
further, and should wait his return from the tavern. A
quarter of an hour elapsed ere he made his appearance, and,
when he did, he looked at me with an expression of sus-
picion and enquiry.

Mr. A.—Well B., what genius was that you introduced
me to; he don't quite seem to belong to your order?

B.—No, he is or was one of your kind, one who
could take a glass or leave it alone; I thought it a good
opportunity of introducing you to a lecture on temperance.

Mr. A.—By Jove! you did that, and I had to pay for
it too.

B. How was that, Mr. A?

Mr. A.—Because your friend C. was very glad to see

a gentleman of my intelligence from the city ; hoped he should meet me again. Was sorry he could not return the treat, as he had left his purse at home, and wound up by insinuating that perhaps I could lend him 50cts. for the occasion. Would be sure to see me with his friend B, &c.

B.—Ah! C., is a smart fellow, and I had an object in making you acquainted with him. I scarcely ever spoke to him before, but I know his history. He used to be able to take it or leave it alone, but now he always takes it and never leaves it alone, if he can get it. Besides, he is no ways scrupulous as to how he gets it. He would borrow ten cents from a blind beggar, if he could. Yet, he was once in the best circumstances, and was looked upon as the soul of honor and spirit.

Mr. A.—My God! what a contrast; how did he come to his present degradation? I should like to have his history.

B.—Well, I will tell you. He came to his present position precisely as thousands do, and began by doing as you are doing now. He was gay and social, and thought he could " take it or leave it alone ;" but as it is a sad case, I shall give you a sketch of his history. Poor C. was the only child of a widow, whose husband died shortly after their marriage. She was married again and lavished all her love and care on her only child. He grew up a handsome boy enough to make any mother proud. He got the best education, and at 24 years of age he was admitted a partner in a respectable business. For years he was apparently prosperous, and was the rage among the young ladies ; while he was the leader in all social boon companionship. He could not be said to neglect his business but his growing irregularities, for they did come, slowly but surely, were beginning to attract attention. At last he married the prettiest girl in the village, a gentle, confiding creature, who adored her husband ! who though vexed and grieved, could not think an occasional case of drunkenness was wrong in him, no matter what it would have been in others. At last his excesses became so great that his partner got quit of him, and headlong precipitation into excess followed. His means were soon dissipated, and just as want was beginning to stare them in the face, his loving little wife. sank broken-hearted into an early grave, leaving one little image of herself to the care of the doubly crazy father. Fortunately the mother's relations took the little stranger, which the besotted father was not loth to surrender, and he went to stay with his now poor old mother, a spiritless, aimless wretch. His downward course was so rapid and so complete that he seemed to think of nothing but how to obtain drink, and under one pretence or another he has contrived to strip his aged mother of nearly all she possessed. Such is the end of the once gay and handsome C., who could then take it or leave it alone. How do you like the picture?

Mr A.—Well, I must confess, it is not very encouraging; but then he is an exceptional case. There are not many such.

B.—Hold there; there are many such. Every drunkard is an instance of a man who could once take it or leave it alone, as I can shew you, if you are not yet convinced.

Mr. A.—Well, B., I own there is great truth in what you have said, and I am half convinced that it is safest to leave it alone; you have introduced me to a pretty good lecture on temperance, at a cost of 50 cents. When I see you next, I shall tell you my decision.

. . . .

DEBATES OF CONSCIENCE

WITH

A DISTILLER, A WHOLESALE DEALER, AND A RETAILER.

DIALOGUE I.

AT THE DISTILLERY.—FIRST INTERVIEW.

DISTILLER.—Good morning, Mr. Conscience; though I know you to be one of the earliest risers, especially of late, I hardly expected to meet you here at day-dawn.

CONSCIENCE.—I am none too early, it seems, to find you at your vocation. But how are you going to dispose of this great black building?

DISTILLER.—Why, I do not understand you.

CONSCIENCE.—What are you doing with these boiling craters, and that hideous worm there?

DISTILLER.—Pray explain yourself.

CONSCIENCE.—Whose grain is that? and what is bread called in the Bible?

DISTILLER.—More enigmatical still.

CONSCIENCE.—To what market do you mean to send that long row of casks? and how many of them will it take upon an average to dig a drunkard's grave?

DISTILLER.—Ah, I understand you now. I was hoping that I had quieted you on that score. But I perceive you have come upon the old errand. You intend to read me another lesson upon the sixth commandment. But what would you have me do?

CONSCIENCE.—Put out these fires.

DISTILLER.—Nay, but hear me. I entered into this business with your approbation. The neighbours all encouraged me. My brethren in the church said it would open a fine market for their rye, and corn, and cider: and even my minister, happening to come along when we were raising, took a little with us under the shade, and said he loved to see his people industrious and enterprising.

CONSCIENCE.—"The times of this ignorance God winked at—but now commandeth all men everywhere to repent." In one part of your defence, at least, you are incorrect. It was not my *voice*, but my *silence*, if any thing, which gave consent; and I have always suspected there was some foul play in the matter, and that I was kept quiet for the time by certain deleterious opiates. Indeed, I distinctly recollect the morning bitters and evening toddy, which you were accustomed to give me; and though I thought but little of it then, I now see that it deadened all my sensibilities. This, I am aware, is no excuse. I ought to have resisted—I ought to have refused, and to have paralyzed the hand which put the cup to my lips. And when you struck the first stroke on this ground, I ought to have warned you off with the voice of seven thunders. That I did not then speak out, and do my duty, will cause me extreme regret and self-reproach to the latest hour of my life.

DISTILLER.—But what, my dear Conscience, has made you all at once so much wiser, not only than your former self, but than hundreds of enlightened men in every community, whose piety was never doubted? I myself know, and have heard of not a few good Christians, including even deacons and elders, who still continue to manufacture ardent spirit, and think, or seem to think it right.

CONSCIENCE.—And think it right! Ask their conscience. I should like to witness some of those interviews which take place in the night, and which make Christian distillers—(what a solecism!)—so much more irritable than they used to be. I know one of the brotherhood, at least, whose conscience has been goading him these five years, and yet he perseveres.

DISTILLER.—But if I stop, what will the people do? Half the farmers in town depend upon their rye and cider to pay their taxes, and even to support the Gospel.

CONSCIENCE.—So, then, you are pouring out these streams of liquid death over the land, and burning up your own neighbours, to enable them to pay their taxes and support religion! Why don't you set up a coffin factory, to create a brisker demand for lumber, and so help the farmers to pay their taxes; and then spread the small-pox among the people, that they may die the faster, and thus increase your business, and give you a fair profit? It will not do. I tell you, that I can give you no peace till you put out these fires and destroy that worm.

DISTILLER.—How can I? Here is all my living, especially since, as you know, my eldest son fell into bad habits, in spite of all the good advice I daily gave him, and squandered what might have afforded me a comfortable independence.

CONSCIENCE.—Suppose you were now in Brazil, and the owner of a large establishment to fit out slave traders with handcuffs for the coast of Africa, and could not change your business without considerable pecuniary sacrifice; would you make the sacrifice, or would you keep your fires and hammers still going?

DISTILLER.—Why do you ask such puzzling questions? You know I don't like them at all, especially when my mind is occupied with other subjects. Leave me, at least till I can compose myself, I beseech you.

CONSCIENCE.—Nay, but hear me through. Is it right for you to go on manufacturing fevers, dropsy, consumption, delirium-tremens, and a host of other frightful diseases, because your property happens to be vested in a distillery? Is it consistent with the great law of love by which you profess to be governed? Will it bear examination in a dying hour? Shall I bid you look back upon it from the brink of eternity, that you may from such recollections gather holy courage for your pending conflict with the king of terrors? Will you bequeath this magazine

of wrath and perdition to your only son not already
ruined, and go out of the world rejoicing that you can
leave the whole concern in the hands of one who is so
trustworthy and so dear ?

[Here the Distiller leaves abruptly, without answering
a word.]

SECOND INTERVIEW.

DISTILLER.—(Seeing Conscience approach, and beginning to tremble.)   What, so soon and so early at your post
again ?   I did hope for a short respite.

CONSCIENCE.—O, I am distressed—I cannot hold my
peace.   I am pained at my very heart.

DISTILLER.—Do be composed, I beseech you, and hear
what I have to say.   Since our last interview I have resolved to sell out, and I expect the purchaser on in a very
few days.

CONSCIENCE.—What will *he* do with the establishment
when he gets it ?

DISTILLER.—You must ask him, and not me.   But
whatever he may do with it, *I* shall be clear.

CONSCIENCE.—I wish I could be sure of that; but let
us see.   Though you will not make poison by the hundred
barrels any longer yourself, you will sell this laboratory of
death to another man, for the same horrid purpose.   You
will not, with your own hands, go on forging daggers for
maniacs to use upon themselves and their friends, provided
you can get some one to take your business at a fair price.
You will no longer drag the car of Juggernaut over the
bodies of prostrate devotees if you can *sell out the privilege
to good advantage !*

DISTILLER.—Was ever any man's conscience so captious before ?   You seem determined not to be satisfied
with anything.   But beware ; by pushing matters in this
way you will produce a violent " reaction."   Even professors
of religion will not bear it.   For myself, I wish to treat
you with all possible respect ; but forbearance itself must
have its limits.

CONSCIENCE.—Possibly you may be able to hold me in check a little longer; but I am all the while gathering strength for an onset which you cannot withstand; and if you cannot bear these kind remonstrances now, how will you grapple with "the worm that never dies?"

DISTILLER.—Enough, enough. I will obey your voice. But why so pale and deathlike?

CONSCIENCE.—O, I am sick, I am almost suffocated. These tartarean fumes, these dreadful forebodings, these heart-rending sights, and above all, my horrid dreams, I cannot endure them. There comes our nearest neighbor, stealing across the lots, with his jug and half-bushel of rye. What is his errand, and where is his hungry shivering family? And see there too, that tattered, half-starved boy, just entering the yard with a bottle—who sent him here at this early hour? All these barrels—where are the wretched beings who are to consume this liquid fire, and to be consumed by it?

DISTILLER.—Spare me, spare me, I beseech you. By going on at this rate a little longer you will make me as nervous as yourself.

CONSCIENCE.—But I cannot close this interview till I have related one of the dreams to which I just alluded. It was only last night that I suffered in this way, more than tongue can tell. The whole terrific vision is written in letters of fire upon the tablet of my memory: and I feel it all the while burning deeper and deeper.

I thought I stood by a great river of melted lava, and while I was wondering from what mountain or vast abyss it came, suddenly the field of my vision was extended to the distance of several hundred miles, and I perceived that, instead of springing from a single source, this rolling torrent of fire was fed by numerous tributary streams, and these again by smaller rivulets. And what do you think I heard and beheld, as I stood petrified with astonishment and horror? There were hundreds of poor wretches struggling and just sinking in the merciless flood. As I contemplated the scene still more attentively, the confused noise of boisterous and profane merriment, mingled with loud shrieks of despair, saluted my ears. The hair of my head stood up— and looking this way and that way, I beheld crowds of men, women, and children, thronging down to the very margin of the river—some eagerly bowing down to slake their thirst with the consuming liquid, and others convulsively striving to hold them back. Some I saw actually pushing their neighbors headlong from the treacherous bank, and others encouraging them to plunge in, by holding up the fiery temptation to their view. To insure a sufficient depth of the river, so that destruction might be made doubly sure, I saw a great number of men, and some whom I knew to be members of the church, laboriously turning their respective contributions of the glowing and hissing liquid into the main channel. This was more than I could bear. I was in perfect torture. But when I expostulated with those who were nearest to the place where I stood, they coolly answered, *This is the way in which we get our living.*

But what shocked me more than all the rest, and curdled every drop of blood in my veins, was the sight which I had of this very distillery pouring out its tributary stream of fire! And O, it distracts, it maddens me to think of it. There you yourself stood feeding the torrent which had already swallowed up some of your own family, and threatened every moment to sweep you away! This last circumstance brought me from the bed, by one convulsive bound, into the middle of the room; and I awoke in an agony which I verily believe I could not have sustained for another moment.

DISTILLER.—I will feed the torrent no longer. The fires of my distillery shall be put out. From this day, from this hour, I renounce the manufacture of ardent spirits for ever.

DIALOGUE II.

WHOLESALE DEALER'S COUNTING-ROOM.

CONSCIENCE.—(Looking over the ledger with a serious air.) What is that last invoice from the West Indies?

RUM-DEALER.—Only a few casks of fourth proof, for particular customers.

CONSCIENCE.—And that domestic poison, via New Orleans; and on the next page, that large consignment, via Erie Canal?

DEALER.—O, nothing but two small lots of prime whiskey, such as we have been selling these twenty years. But why these chiding inquiries? They disquiet me exceedingly. And to tell you the plain truth, I am more than half offended at this morbid inquisitiveness.

CONSCIENCE.—Ah, I am afraid, as I have often told you, that this is a bad business; and the more I think of it, the more it troubles me.

DEALER.—Why so? You are always preaching up industry as a Christian virtue, and my word for it, were I to neglect my business, and saunter about the hotels and steamboat wharves, as some do, you would fall into convulsions, as if I had committed the unpardonable sin.

CONSCIENCE.—Such pettish quibbling is utterly unworthy of your good sense and ordinary candor. You know, as well as I do, the great difference between industry in some safe and honest calling, and driving a business which carries poverty and ruin to thousands of families.

DEALER.—*Honest* industry! This is more cruel still. You have known me too long to throw out such insinuations; and besides, it is notorious, that some of the first merchants in our city are engaged, far more extensively, in the same traffic.

CONSCIENCE.—Be it so. "To their own Master they stand or fall." But if fair dealing consists in "doing as we would be done by," how can a man of your established mercantile and Christian reputation sustain himself, if he continues to deal in an article which he knows to be more destructive than all the plagues of Egypt ?

DEALER.—Do you intend, then, to make me answerable for all the mischief that is done by ardent spirit, in the whole State and nation ?   What I sell is a mere drop of the bucket, compared with the consumption of a single county.   Where is the proof that the little which my respectable customers carry into the country, with their other groceries, ever does any harm ?   How do you know that it helps to make such a frightful host of drunkards and vagabonds ?   And if it did, whose fault would it be ? I never gave nor sold a glass of whiskey to a tippler in my life.   Let those who will drink to excess, and make brutes of themselves, answer for it.

CONSCIENCE.—Yes, certainly *they* must answer for it ; but will that excuse those who furnish the poison ?   Did you never hear of abettors and accessories, as well as principals in crime?   When Judas, in all the agony of remorse and despair, threw down the thirty pieces of silver before the chief priests and elders, exclaiming, *I have sinned, in that I have betrayed the innocent blood*—they coolly answered, *What is that to us? See thou to that.*   And was it therefore nothing to them ?   Had they no hand in that cruel tragedy?   Was it nothing to Pilate—nothing to Herod—nothing to the multitude who were consenting to the crucifixion of the Son of God—because they did not drive the nails and thrust the spear ?

O, when I think of what you are doing to destroy the bodies and souls of men, I cannot rest.   It terrifies me at all hours of the night.   Often and often, when I am just losing myself in sleep, I am startled by the most frightful groans and unearthly imprecations, coming out of these hogsheads.   And then, those long processions of rough-made coffins and beggared families, which I dream of, from nightfall till daybreak, they keep me all the while in a cold sweat, and I can no longer endure them.

DEALER.—Neither can I.   Something must be done, You have been out of your head more than half the time for this six months. I have tried all the ordinary remedies upon you without the least effect. Indeed, every new remedy seems only to aggravate the disease. O, what would not I give for the discovery of some anodyne which would lay these horrible phantasms. The case would be infinitely less trying, if I could sometimes persuade you, for a night or two, to let me occupy a different appartment from yourself for—when your spasms come on, one might as well try to sleep with embers in his bosom, as where you are.

CONSCIENCE.—Would it mend the matter at all, if, instead of sometimes dreaming, I were to be always wide awake?

DEALER.—Ah, there's the grand difficulty. For I find that when you do wake up, you are more troublesome than ever. *Then* you are always harping upon my being a professor of religion, and bringing up some text of Scripture, which might as well be let alone, and which you would not ring in my ears, if you had any regard to my peace, or even your own. More than fifty times, within a month, have you quoted, "*By their fruits ye shall know them.*" In fact, so uncharitable have you grown of late‘ that from the drift of some of your admonitions, a stranger would think me but little, if any, better than a murderer. And all because some vagabond or other may possibly happen to shorten his days by drinking a little of the identical spirit which passes through my hands.

CONSCIENCE.—You do me bare justice when you say that I have often reproved you, and more earnestly of late, than I formerly did. But my remonstrances have always been between you and me alone. If I have charged you with the guilt of hurrying men to the grave and to hell, by this vile traffic, it has not been upon the house-top. I cannot, it is true, help knowing how it grieves your brethren, gratifies the enemies of religion, and excites the scorn of drunkards themselves, to see your wharf covered with the fiery element; but I speak only in your own ears. To yourself I have wished to prove a faithful monitor, though

I have sad misgivings, at times, even with regard to that. You will bear me witness, however, that I have sometimes trembled exceedingly, for fear that I should be compelled, at last, to carry the matter up by indictment to the tribunal of eternal Justice.

To avoid this dreadful necessity, let me once more reason the case with you in a few words. You know perfectly well, that ardent spirit kills its tens of thousands in this Dominion every year : and there is no more room to doubt that many of these lives are destroyed by the very liquor which you sell, then if you saw them staggering under it into the drunkards' grave. How then can you possibly throw off bloodguiltiness, with the light which you now enjoy ? In faithfulness to your soul, and to Him whose viceregent I am, 1 cannot say less, especially if you persist any longer in the horrible traffic.

DEALER.—Pardon me, my dear Conscience, if, under the excitement of the moment, I complained of your honest and continued importunity. Be assured, there is no friend in the world with whom I am so desirous of maintaining a good understanding as with yourself. And for your relief and satisfaction, I now give you my solemn pledge, that I will close up this branch of my business as soon as possible. Indeed, I have commenced the process already. My last consignments are less, by more than one half, than were those of the preceding years ; and I intend that, when another year comes about, my books shall speak still more decidedly in my favor.

CONSCIENCE.—These resolutions would be perfectly satisfactory, if they were in the *present tense*. But if it was wrong to sell five hundred casks last year, how can it be right to sell two hundred this year, and one hundred next ? If it is criminal to poison forty men at one time, how can it be innocent to poison twenty at another ? If you may not throw a hundred firebrands into the city, how will you prove that you may throw one ?

DEALER.—Very true, very true—but let us waive this point for the present. It affects me very strangely.

CONSCIENCE.—How long, then, will it take to dry up this fountain of death?

DEALER.—Don't call it so, I beseech you; but I intend to be entirely out of the business in two or three years, at farthest.

CONSCIENCE.—Two or three years! Can you, then, after all that has passed between us, persist two or three years longer in a contraband traffic? I verily thought, that when we had that long conference two or three months ago, you resolved to close the concern at once; and that when we parted, I had as good as your promise, that you would. Surely, you cannot so soon have forgotten it.

DEALER.—No, I remember that interview but too well; for I was never so unhappy in my life. I did almost resolve, and more than half promise, as you say. But after I had time to get a little composed, I thought you had pushed matters rather too far; and that I could convince you of it, at a proper time. I see, however, that the attempt would be fruitless. But as I am anxious for a compromise, let me ask whether, if I give away all the profits of this branch of my business to the Bible Society, and other institutions, till I can close it up, you will not be satisfied?

CONSCIENCE.—Let me see. Five hundred dollars, or one hundred dollars, earned to promote the cause of religion by selling poison! By killing husbands, and fathers, and brothers, and torturing poor women and children! It smells of blood—and can God possibly accept of such an offering?

DEALER.—So then, it seems, I must stop the sale at once, or entirely forfeit what little charity you have left.

CONSCIENCE.—You must. Delay is death—death to the consumer at least; and how can you flatter yourself that it will not prove your own eternal death? My convictions are decisive, and be assured, I deal thus plainly because I love you, and cannot bear to become your everlasting tormentor.

DIALOGUE III.

AT THE RETAILER'S STAND.

CONSCIENCE.—Do you know that little half-starved, bare-footed child, that you just sent home with two quarts of rank poison?

(Retailer hums a tune to himself, and affects not to hear the question.)

CONSCIENCE.—I see by the paper of this morning, that the furniture of Mr. M——is to be sold under the hammer to-morrow. Have I not often seen him in your tap-room?

RETAILER.—I am extremely busy just now, in bringing up my ledger.

CONSCIENCE.—Have you heard how N——abused his family, and turned them all into the street the other night, after being supplied by you with whiskey?

RETAILER.—He is a *brute*, and ought to be confined in a dungeon six months at least, upon bread and water.

CONSCIENCE.—Was not S——, who hung himself lately, one of your steady customers? and where do you think his soul is now fixed for eternity? You sold him rum that evening, not ten minutes before you went to the prayer-meeting, and had his money in your pocket—for you would not trust him—when you led in the exercises. I heard you ask him once, why he did not attend meeting, and send his children to the Sabbath-school; and I shall never forget his answer. "Come, you talk like a minister; but, after all, we are about of one mind—at least in some things. Let me have my jug and be going."

RETAILER.—I know he was an impudent, hardened wretch; and though his death was extremely shocking, I am glad to be rid of him.

CONSCIENCE.—Are you ready to meet him at the bar of God, and to say to the Judge. "He was my neighbor —I saw him going down the broad way, and I did every thing that a Christian could do to save him?"

5

RETAILER.—(Aside. O that I could stifle the upbraidings of this cruel monitor.) You keep me in constant torment. This everlasting cant about *rank poison, and liquid fire, and blood, and murder,* is too much far even a Christian to put up with. Why, if any body but Conscience were to make such insinuations and charges, he would be indictable as a foul slanderer, before a court of justice.

CONSCIENCE.—Is it *slander,* or is it *because I tell you the truth,* that your temper is so deeply ruffled under my remonstrances? Suppose I were to hold my peace, while your hands are becoming more and more deeply crimsoned with this bloody traffic. What would you say to me, when you come to meet that poor boy who just went out, and his drunken father, and broken-hearted mother, at the bar of God? Would you thank your conscience for having let you alone while there was space left for repenttance?

RETAILER.—Ah, had honest trader ever *such* a conscience to deal with before? Always just so uncompromising —always talking about the "golden rule"—always insisting upon a moral standard which nobody can live up to— always scenting poverty, murder, and suicide, in every glass of whiskey, though it were a mile off. The truth is, you are not fit to live in this world at all. Acting in conformity with your more than puritanical rules, would starve any man and his family to death.

CONSCIENCE.—Well, here comes another customer— see the carbuncles! Will you fill his bottle with wrath, to be poured out without mixture, by and by, upon your own head? Do you not know that his pious wife is extremely ill, and suffering for want of every comfort, in their miserable cabin?

RETAILER.—No, Mr. E——, go home and take care of your family. I am determined to harbor no more drunkards here.

CONSCIENCE.—You mean to make a distinction then, do you, between harboring those who are already ruined, and helping to destroy such as are now respectable members of society. You will not hereafter tolerate a single *drunkard* on your premises; but—

RETAILER.—Ah, I see what you are aiming at; and really it is too much for any honest man, and, still more for any Christian to bear. You know it is a long time since I have pretended to answer half your captious questions. There's no use in it. It only leads on to others still more impertinent and puzzling. If I am the hundredth part of that factor of Satan which you would make me, I ought to be dealt with, and cast out of the church at once; and why don't my good brethren see to it?

CONSCIENCE.—That's a hard question, which they, perhaps, better know how to answer than I do.

RETAILER.—But have you forgotten, my good Conscience, that in retailing spirit, I am under the immediate eye and sanction of the laws. Mine is no contraband traffic, as you very well know. I hold a license from the rulers and fathers of the state, and have paid my money for it into the public treasury. Why do they continue to grant and sell licenses, if it is wrong for me to sell rum?

CONSCIENCE.—Another hard question, which I leave them to answer as best they can. It is said, however, that public bodies have no soul, and if they have no soul, it is difficult to see how they can have any conscience; and if not, what should hinder them from selling licenses? but suppose the civil authorities should offer to sell you a license to keep a gambling-house, or a brothel, would you purchase such a license, and present it as a salve to your conscience?

RETAILER.—I tell you once more, there is no use in trying to answer your questions; for say what I will, you have the art of turning everything against me. It was not always so, as you must very distinctly remember. Formerly I could retail hogshead after hogshead of all kinds of spirits, and you slept as quietly as a child. But since you began to read these Reports and Tracts about drinking, and to attend Temperance meetings, I have scarcely had an hour's peace of my life. I feared that something like this would be the effect upon your nervous temperament, when you began; and you may recollect that I strongly objected to your troubling yourself with these new speculations. It now grieves me to think that I ever yielded to your importunity; and beware that you do not push me to extremities in this matter, for I have about come to the resolution that I will have no more of these mischievous pamphlets, either about my store or tavern; and that your temperance agents may declaim to to the winds and walls, if they please.

CONSCIENCE.—I am amazed at your blindness and obstinacy. It is now from three to five years since I began to speak—though in a kind of indistinct undertone at first—against this bloody traffic. I have reasoned, I have remonstrated, and latterly I have threatened and implored with increasing earnestness. At times you have listened, and been convinced that the course which you are pursuing, in this day of light, is infamous, and utterly inconsistent with a Christian profession; but before your convictions and resolutions have time to ripen into action, the love of *money* regains its ascendency; and thus have you gone on *resolving, and relapsing, and re-resolving*—one hour at the preparatory lecture, and the next unloading whiskey at your door; one moment mourning over the prevalence of intemprance, and the next arranging your decanters to entice the simple; one day partaking of the cup of the Lord at his table, and the next offering the cup of devils to your neighbors; one day singing,

> "All that I have, and all I am,
> I consecrate to Thee,"

and the next, *for the sake of a little gain,* sacrificing your character, and polluting all you can induce to drink! O, how can I hold my peace? How can I let you alone? If you will persist, your blood, and the blood of those whom you thus entice and destroy, be upon your own head.

Whether you will hear, or whether you will forbear, I shall not cease to remonstrate ; and when I can do no more to reclaim you, I will sit down at your gate, in the bitterness of despair, and cry, *Murder !* MURDER !! MURDER !!!

RETAILER.—(Pale and trembling.) "Go thy way for this time ; when I have a convenient season, I will call for thee."

THE DRUNKARD'S DAUGHTER.

BY MR. J. E. MCCONAUGHY.

Characters.

STELLA.	RUTH.
HATTIE.	LUCY.
OLIVE.	SUSAN.

SCHOOL-GIRLS.

SCENE I.

*A school play-ground.—Enter Stella, Olive, Lucy,
and Ruth.*

STELLA.—You may say what you please, girls, I will
never consent to have Harriet Cook invited to our picnic;
it is to be quite a select affair, and I for one do not choose
to associate with drunkard's children. She has no business in our school at all. The public school is the place
for her—mother says so. She is surprised that Miss
Harrington takes her.

LUCY.—But it is no fault of hers, Stella, that her father drinks; I am sure she is one of the nicest, sweetest
girls in school, and one of the best scholars too. I am
sure she has helped you often enough over your arith-
metic, to have you speak more kindly of her.

STELLA.—Dear me! I do not know that I am obliged
to associate with her as an equal on that account. My
father is very particular whom I associate with. You

ought to have seen old Jimmy Cook staggering home the other night; he went past our house with a pack of boys following him, pulling his hair and teasing him in every way they could. It was funny to see him clutch after them, and try to strike them; but the boys were too quick for him. They only shouted and laughed, and told him to try again. I laughed till I cried, and father came and stood beside me, and laughed too, as heartily as I did.

OLIVE.—Poor, poor Hattie! I do hope she did not see him.

STELLA.—But she did, I know, for I saw her on the opposite side of the street, hurrying on with her vail pulled over her face. I hoped she would not put on quite so many airs after it, and think herself as good as any body else, but it don't seem to have done her much good.

OILVE.—(*Indignantly.*) For shame, Stella! Have you no heart? As if it was the poor girl's fault; and as for putting on airs, that is what Hattie never does; she only maintains a decent self-respect, if she does carry an aching heart in her breast. We should be careful about rejoicing over the misfortunes of another, for trouble may come to us when we look for it the least.

STELLA.—Dear me, what a croaker! I presume now she expects my father to turn drunkard, and go reeling through the streets, just because I laughed at Jimmy Cook. *My father* is a gentleman, and would never stoop to anything so degrading as to drink low, poisoned liquors. He never has anything but the finest wines on his side-board, and they are often four or five dollars a bottle.

RUTH.—But people can become intemperate just as well on wine as on whiskey. It is not a whit less dangerous.

STELLA.—Suppose you set up for a temperance lecturer; you know it is quite a fashion for ladies to lecture. You are tall and good-looking, and a good elocutionist, and I know you would make quite a sensation.

RUTH.—My first point will be, then, to urge you all to

be kind to the drunkard's children. By all means let us ask Hattie to our picnic, and make the day as bright as we can for her.

STELLA.—(*Much offended.*) Then you will have to dispense with *my* company, I assure you.

RUTH.—We will try and bear it with as much resignation as possible.

STELLA.—You are very sarcastic, Miss Davis; but I can tell you, mother shall not send the elegant basket of cake she has prepared for it, nor a single strawberry from our vines.

OLIVE.—Oh! don't worry about that, dear; we have more strawberries and cake promised than we can possibly use. But, Stella, think better of it, and come, you'll lose so much pleasure, and you know you needn't speak a word to Hattie if you don't want to. Only don't treat her rudely, for that is very wrong, and I know it would offend half the girls in school; they all love Hattie.

STELLA.—(*Leaving angrily.*) They are welcome to— a drunkard's daughter, indeed! I think things have come to a pretty pass in our school when she is preferred before a *gentleman's* daughter.

RUTH.—Worth before station any time, Stella. (*Exit Stella, slamming the door.*)

LUCY.—You were almost too hard, Ruth.

RUTH.—I know it, but her airs are unendurable. But, poor girl, she may see sorrow herself, before many days. Her father spends nearly all his evenings at the club, and plays and takes wine most immoderately. I do not think she suspects such a thing as that he can possibly be in danger. But girls, we must make haste, for I see Miss Harrington coming up the walk. She likes to have us all in our places as soon as the bell rings. (*Exit girls— a bell ringing.*)

SCENE II.

Recitation Room.—Hattie, Olive, Lucy weaving wreaths for the picnic.

OLIVE.—Hattie, please help me twine in this myrtle; I can never get it to suit myself, but your fingers have the knack of making every thing fit in right.

HATTIE.—I think you are doing very well, Olive, but I will help you if I can. There, how will that please you? How lovely those carnations are! Look, girls. (*She fits the wreath on Olive's head.*)

LUCY.—It is perfect. Don't stir a leaf, Hattie. But here comes Susan Lee. Do, pray, girls, be careful what you say, she does make so much trouble repeating things; and it seems to me nothing ever goes on that she doesn't know.

(*Enter Susan.*)

SUSAN.—There, girls, are all the flowers I had time to gather. Mother sent me over to Mrs. Nippers' to get the particulars of that awful affair that's just happened, and I was tired clear out when I came home.

GIRLS.—What awful affair? Do tell us! Anybody killed?

SUSAN.—Well, not quite, I suppose, but pretty near. It all happened at that club, which was thought to be such a wonderfully aristocratic affair. Stella's father, you know, is called one of the best players at cards in town; nobody ever beats him. But it happened that he was playing with a gentleman who had not been very long in the club, and they say he lost and lost, oh! I can't tell you how much money; but the more he lost the more angry he got, and risked larger and larger sums, until the man swept all his property. Then he told the man he was a cheat and a liar, and they came to blows. You know Stella's father is a large, strong man, and the other was very slight, so he was very much hurt before any one could or would interfere. Some people say the man will die, but I can't pretend to say. But one thing we are sure of, Mr. Rosylin is safe in jail and I guess Stella won't hold her head quite so high, and lord it over the rest of us quite so much as she used to.

OLIVE.—Hush, Susan, do, Don't let us speak hard things of her, now she is in such trouble. I am sure I pity her with all my heart.

HATTIE.—Poor Stella! I would do any thing in the world I could to comfort her.

SUSAN.—I guess it would comfort her the most never to see the face of one of us again. You certainly don't owe her any good-will, Hattie, of all the rest.

HATTIE.—I am sure I have not the slightest ill-will towards her, and am truly sorry for her trouble; most likely the story is much exaggerated.

SUSAN.—Most likely the half is not known.

LUCY.—Well, whatever the truth proves to be, girls, we will always treat Stella as kindly as ever; for, whatever she may have maintained to the contrary, children are not responsible for the faults of their parents. They may suffer for them, but they are not to blame for them. But now we must gather up our wreaths, girls, for the carriages are coming, and we can finish them in the woods. (*Exeunt. omnes.*)

WHITE LIES.

—

Characters.

MR. CARR.   HORACE.   MARK.

HORACE.—Father, what is a *white* lie?

MR. CARR.—There is no such thing, Horace. A lie is always black and wicked.

MARK.—But, Father, I have heard people talk about white lies, too.

HORACE.—When Harry Howell had his cousin to tea last week, he told us he had a large party, and when we found him out, he said it was only a white lie, anyhow.

MARK.—And Mr. Haynes, when he said the old rooster he sold last market day was a young chicken, said it was only a *white* lie.

MR. CARR.—What is a lie, Horace?

HORACE.—A false statement, intended to deceive; you told us that, long ago.

MR. CARR.—What was Harry Howell's statement, and that of Mr. Haynes? True statements?

HORACE.—No sir; they were false.

MR. CARR.—Intended to deceive?

HORACE.—Yes sir.

MR. CARR.—Then they were lies! Never try to soothe your conscience with such mistaken ideas, as that the magnitude or importance of a lie, makes any difference in its guilt. A half lie, or quarter of a lie, is as bad as a whole one. Remember that.

MARK.—But, father, many boys who would not tell a deliberate falsehood, will twist the truth, or evade it, to deceive a little bit.

MR. CARR.—That is just as bad.

HORACE.—It is very cowardly.

MR. CARR.—If a boy does anything wrong, intentionally or accidentally, through carelessness, perhaps, or because he was ignorant of the consequences of his fault, and then tries to shuffle out of his scrape by evasion or deceit, he is as guilty of falsehood, as if he had made a direct denial of his guilt. He doubles the burden on his conscience, by adding to his first fault the sin of lying.

HORACE.—But, father, our teacher is so very strict, that the boys, many of them, are afraid to own a fault.

MR. CARR.—Is he less strict, when he finds he has been deceived?

MARK.—Indeed he is not?

MR. CARR.—Then the penalty is greater, as well as the sin.

HORACE.—Some of the boys look mean enough when he catches them in an untruth.

MARK.—But, father, are not exaggerations, stories made up about people, little incidents magnified into great events, white lies?

MR. CARR.—No, Mark. When the line is passed, by even a hair's breadth, that divides truth from falsehood, there is no shading of difference in the grades of that falsehood. What is not true is false, and a lie is a lie, be it big or little, important or trivial.

MARK.—But you would not like to say that a person who simply exaggerates is a liar?

MR. CARR.—Yes; such is the truth. A person who habitually indulges in exaggeration or story-telling is mean and worthless, despicable both to his fellow-men and in the eyes of his Maker.

HORACE.—And I have noticed, too, father, when they once pass the barrier of truth, that they keep adding lie to lie, till they are so entangled that they must be detected.

MR. CARR.—It is certainly much easier to speak the truth, than to invent even the most plausible falsehood.

Strive, my sons, always to guard against the least deviation from the exact truth. Nothing is more beautiful than a truthful boy, and you will find no one more respected.

MARK.—That is so. I do not believe you could torture Leon Henderson into telling a lie, and all the boys respect him, though some of them pretend to sneer at him.

HORACE.—And our teacher will take his word against the strongest circumstantial evidence.

MR. CARR.—How proud his father must be of such a boy!

HORACE.—We will try, father, to give you the same cause for pride.

MARK.—We will indeed, father.

MR. CARR.—Do so, my boys. Be truthful, candid, and above deceit. Never try to palliate falsehood by thinking it is not so bad as it might me. All lies are alike, and above all, recollect that in the sight of God, there are no *white* lies. [*Curtain falls.*

THE TRIAL OF ALCOHOL.

—

CHARGED WITH MURDER, ROBBERY, &C.

—

Supreme Court of Public Opinion.

The People ⎫
  vs.   ⎬
Alcohol. ⎭

Hon. R. Candor, *Chief Justice.*
Hon. S. Impartiality, ⎫
Hon. G. Patience, ⎬ *Associate Justices.*
Hon. H. Honesty. ⎭

Counsel for the People—J. Goodwill, Att'y Gen.

Council for Defendant—Squire Self-Interest.

The jury, twelve good men, being sworn, the prisoner was brought to the bar, and the Clerk read the Indictment.

Clerk.—May it please the Court, the Indictment charges the prisoner—

1.—With swindling and taking money under false pretences.
2.—With being a frequenter of gambling houses and other vile places, and a great cause there of disorder and crime.
3.—With being a family disturber, breaking up domestic peace and happiness.
4.—Depriving many men of their reason, and causing them to commit suicide.
5.—Reducing many families to pauperism and shame.
6.—Causing a thousand murders every year, and filling up poorhouses and mad-houses with ruined victims.
7.—With opposing the blessed gospel and dragging many souls to death and hell.

Prisoner, what is your plea, guilty or not guilty?

Prisoner.—Not guilty.

CLERK.—How will you be tried?

PRISONER.—By God and my country.

CLERK.—God send you a good deliverance.

ATTORNEY GENERAL.—May it please the Court and Gentlemen of the Jury, the prisoner is charged with a variety of heinous crimes—with being a disturber of the public peace, a seducer, a robber, a murderer, both of the bodies and the souls of men. I shall not detain you with a long speech, but substantiate the truths of the indictment by good and true witnesses. I first call Mr. Easymind.

Mr. Easymind do you know the prisoner? Can you tell anything about him?

WITNESS.—I can, Sir; for I have suffered much from him. He was often at my father's house and he professed much medical skill, and when my wife was sick, he promised a cure, but made her a drunkard and I forbade him my house.

ATT'Y GEN.—Have you any sons?

WITNESS.—Yes, Sir, three; but I have not much comfort in them, for they are constantly drawn away by the prisoner to scenes of drinking, horse-racing and gambling.

ATT'Y GEN.—How do they come home?

WITNESS.—Often drunk at the midnight hour.

SQUIRE SELF-INTEREST.—You say he made your wife a drunkard. Do you know he did? Remember, Sir, you are on your oath.

WITNESS.—Why if he didn't, who did?

SQUIRE S. I.—That is not answering the question. Do you know he made her a drunkard? Can you swear she was not born one?

WITNESS.—I know that she was not one till she began to take his medicines.

SQUIRE S. I.—You say he ruined your sons; were they not vicious before they became acquainted with him?

WITNESS.—No, Sir; never were better boys.

ATT'Y GEN.—Mr. Sobermind, do you know the prisoner at the bar?

WITNESS.—I once did, to my sorrow. He found me an industrious, hard-labouring young man. He took me to the tavern, the store, the saloon—I tremble to think what he did for me. He got all my money out of my pockets, and my clothes from my back. I became under his leadings a vile drunkard, and slept in barns and behind barrels; but I quit him, Sir, and since then I have come up to be again what I was.

ATT'Y GEN.—What does he do with families?

WITNESS.—It would take me a year to tell the sorrow and trouble he gives.

ATT'Y GEN.—Did you ever know him to divide husband and wife?

WITNESS.—Yes, Sir, in many cases.

ATT'Y GEN.—Did he ever cause a murder in your neighborhood?

WITNESS.—Yes, Sir, in many cases. But we could never get him indicted and tried because he had so many friends.

SQUIRE S. I.—You say you are now his enemy.

WITNESS.—Yes, Sir. And if I could get him expelled from the country I would.

SQUIRE S. I.—May it please the Court, I object to this witness. He testifies under strong hostility, and he cannot be expected to speak the truth. His testimony should not be received by the jury.

ATT'Y GEN.—Squire Coke, you have been at the bar many years; what do you know of the prisoner?

WITNESS.—I know that, but for him we lawyers should soon starve.

ATT'Y GEN.—Please explain what you mean.

WITNESS.—Mean? I mean what I say; for more than two-thirds of our criminal cases are caused by him; nearly all the fights and murders are his work.

SQUIRE S. I.—Did he not keep you, by all the votes

he cast, from being a Congressman? Did not all the rum men go against you?

WITNESS.—Yes, Sir. And it was the proudest day of my life.

SQUIRE S. I.—Gentlemen of the Jury, you see under what influence he testifies. His testimony is good for nothing.

ATT'Y GEN.—Mr. Lovetruth, you have been a collector of taxes; what has the prisoner had to do with the taxation of the town?

WITNESS.—He has caused more than one half of it. We have twenty-five paupers all charged to him, and a jail full, and many casualties by fire and wrecks are caused by him for which the town must pay. And since no restraint has been laid upon him, the taxes have been increased double.

SQUIRE S. I.—Do you suppose there would be no taxes among Cold Water men? How much did the Croton Water Works cost?

WITNESS FOR THE DEFENCE.

SQUIRE S. I.—Mr. Animal Appetite, please state what you know of this gentleman.

WITNESS.—He is the best friend I ever had, Sir. He always gives me good cheer and cures me of all my diseases. I could not live without him.

ATT'Y GEN.—Did he never kill any body?

WITNESS.—That is no concern of mine, Sir. Roast beef and plum pudding will kill men if they eat too much.

SQUIRE S. I.—I would call, may it please the Court, upon Mr. Lovegain. What is the influence of this gentleman upon the trade of the country?

WITNESS.—Oh, it has increased it mightily, Sir. We have made more money by this gentleman, than by any cotton speculation or anything else. His liquor draws out more money than all the cotton and tobacco together.

6

ATT'Y GEN.—And what does he give for the money he gets? Anything valuable?

WITNESS.—That's nothing to me, Sir.

ATT'Y GEN.—Is he not then a thief and a robber?

May it please the Court, you have heard all the witnesses for the defence, and they amount to nothing. I shall now, without argument, submit the case.

CHIEF JUSTICE CANDOR charges the Jury—

Gentlemen of the Jury: You have heard the Indictment and the witnesses for and against him. You will render a verdict according to your consciences. I commit the fate of the prisoner to you.

When the Jury came in the Clerk said—

Foreman, what is your verdict—guilty or not guilty?

FOREMAN.—Guilty?

SENTENCE OF THE COURT.

JUDGE—Mr. Prisoner, stand up. You are pronounced guilty of the enormous charges which have been brought against you, and you will be taken hence from the place whence you came, in rum puncheons, and there be cast into a vat of Cold Water. And may you die and be forgotten forever.

A PLEA FOR THE PLEDGE.

JOHN.—There is much talk about Temperance Societies; but I think few people quite understand them, except those who are members thereof. I am not quite sure that I am well informed on the subject, and as you are a member, perhaps you will be good enough to explain what a Temperance Society is.

THOMAS.—With pleasure. It consists of a number of persons who have agreed not to use alcoholic drinks, who have signed a pledge to that effect, and have formed themselves into a Society to strengthen each other's hands, and to induce others to follow their example.

JOHN.—But why give up the drink altogether? Can not men take it or leave it alone? It is the abuse, not the use, that does the harm, is it not?

THOMAS.—The use, as it is called, leads to the abuse. Drunkenness is only the result of drinking. Our country abounds with sad proofs of this.

JOHN.—But do you mean to say that men can be strong, do their work, and bear fatigue and exposure as well without the drink as with it?

THOMAS.—There is no doubt about it now, at least among those who are properly informed on the subject. The brick-makers, anchor-smiths, harvest-men, etc., in various parts, have tried it and succeeded admirably.

JOHN.—But all who drink do not become drunkards.

THOMAS.—Truly; nor do all gamblers lose their money and character, but many of them do; and as there is great danger of my doing so, therefore I abstain. Besides, what can be done better without, should be avoided, especially when the doing it might involve me and others in trouble.

JOHN.—I think your temperance people make too much of drink; you say there are not less than sixty thousand drunkards in the land, and that about sixty thousand die every year.

THOMAS.—This may seem a very strong statement, but it is only doubted by those who love the drink, and have taken little pains to get at the facts.

JOHN.—Then you say that at least one hundred millions of money are spent, directly and indirectly, in this drink. Now think of that enormous sum! It can not be.

THOMAS.—It's all very well for you to say it can not be; but that assertion has never yet been called in question by any competent authority. Allow me to say I do not think you are one.

JOHN.—But if so many persons were made drunkards every year, should we not have many more of them about than there are?

THOMAS.—Thousands of them are imprisoned for crime, and thousands more shut up in lunatic asylums. They are a short-lived race and die off quickly.

JOHN.—Then what becomes of their wives, widows, and families?

THOMAS.—Why, in many cases, they become a town charge, while in others they are taken care of by their friends and the benevolent public. The pauperism of this country, from drink, is fearful.

JOHN.—What is a pauper?

THOMAS.—A person who, being unable to procure food, clothes, and shelter, is provided with them by the taxpayers.

JOHN.—But do you not think you ·are too hard upon the drink when you say it produces seven-tenths of the crime of this country?

THOMAS.—No. Facts prove it; and facts are stubborn things. Besides, who ought to be better informed on these matters than the judges of the land? They confirm this opinion.

JOHN.—If Temperance Societies have done so much good as you and your friends say they have, how is it that all good people do not join you?

THOMAS.—Because prejudice, appetite, custom, and interest withold the light from them. They are *human*, and therefore err. But there is much improvement in this respect, and we must hope on.

JOHN.—When and where were the Temperance Societies first instituted?

THOMAS.—About fifty years ago in this country of reforms. They first merely rejected ardent spirits, but now we have grafted the teetotal principle on to their anti-spirit system.

JOHN.—Before we part, there is one other point on which I wish to have a little information. I do not like your pledge. If people choose to abstain, why not do so without a pledge? It seems so unmanly.

THOMAS.—It is just the contrary, and gives proof that he who has hitherto been carried away by his appetite and by the customs of society, has at last awakened to the dignity of independence and manhood, and asserted his determination to be *free*. That is manly.

JOHN.—But does not taking a pledge destroy moral freedom and responsibility?

THOMAS.—Certainly not; no more than engagements and pledges of any other kind. It has proved a great boon to many a poor drunkard, who, struggling with innumerable temptations within and around him, has thus, by God's blessing, been enabled to abstain; perhaps, at first, only *because he had pledged himself;* but afterward continued, because he saw it was right to do so. But while I am on this point, excuse me one moment longer while I say, that of all the means of deliverance and of safety in this our probationary state, if any one in God's revealed word stands out in bolder relief than another, it is the system of pledges, covenants, and promises. He has given it His sanction by His examples, entering into solemn covenant with many, and giving pledges for its fulfilment. So also the patriarchs, and prophets, and apostles, and kings, and people, throughout the Scriptures, are to be found uniting in pledges and covenants; and *invariably without exception*, when these pledges and covenants for good objects have been kept, the blessing of God has attended them. (*Exit.*)

THE TRY COMPANY.

BY REV. G. BOWLER.

———

[*James lounging on the stage, whittling. Enter, Samuel.*]

SAMUEL.—Hallo! Jemmy; come, let's go down to old Rogers, and help him to get in his wood. You know how old he is, and he can't do much---let's go down and help him.

JAMES.—Oh! I can't; it's too hard work getting in wood; besides, I'd rather sit still than work, any time.

SAMUEL.—Yes, but you know that the more you sit still, the more we want to; and if we never stir our stumps, we shall never get to be anything in the world. For my part, I want to be somebody, and I mean to be. Come! come along; let's go and help the old man.

JAMES.—No, I can't I don't want to help other folks. It's as much as I can do to help myself; besides, I've got lots of work to do at home—wood to split and coal to sift, and and all sorts of things. You may go if you're a mind to, but I shan't.

SAMUEL.—Well, Jemmy, if you've got work to do of your own, I won't urge you; but I thought as you sat here whittling, that you had nothing else to do. I shouldn't think that was the way to get work done up.

JAMES.—Oh, well; I don't like to work. I wish there wasn't any such thing as work. This pushing, and pulling, and working, and studying, aint the thing I like; besides, I never can make anything go. My wood is always full of knots, and I can never find the axe when I want it; and if I try to dig in the garden, it's always full of stones and old roots; and I aint agoing to trouble myself about work, now I tell ye.

SAMUEL.—Well, Jemmy, I can't stop to talk with you now, for we boys are going to form a Try Company, and after that we shall get in old Roger's wood for him. I think the best thing you can do will be to join us, and see if you can't wake up a little, and find out how to make work seem like play. You'd better believe that's a good deal pleasanter than 't is to lounge round all day, and say, I can't work, and I don't want to do this and that. Here come the boys, now —some of the wide-awake ones.

[*Enter Hiram and William with sashes on.*]

HIRAM.—Hallo! Sam; I'm glad you're on hand so early, and Jim, too—I didn't expect to see him here; but if he's going to break up his old grumbling habits and join our Try Company, I'm glad to have him—the more the merrier, you know.

JAMES.—Oh, you needn't trouble yourself about me, Hiram; I've no notion of joining your Try Company. What's the use of trying, when there's so many things to do that a fellow can't count 'em? I'm just agoing to let everything slide, and I guess it'll be all the same a hundred years from now.

WILLIAM.—I guess it won't be all the same a hundred years from now, James; for you know the more a man does for himself, the more he is able to do; and if his strength is increased by labor, so is his happiness increased as the fruit of his labor. Besides we haven't got to do everything at once. If we look at all kinds of work at once. it may seem hard. You know when they were building the big chimney over at the glass house, the masons laid only one brick at a time, and it wasn't long before the whole were laid. A man can't jump over a mountain, but if he keeps on, taking one step at a time, he will soon get over it. So I've made up my mind to belong to the Try Company, and if I can't do everything at once, I'll just do one thing at a time, and so in time I'll get all done that I want to do.

HIRAM.—Well, Sam, you know you're to be corporal: now what's the order of the day?

SAMUEL.—Well, we must have material to form a company out of, so I've appointed John Green and William Brown recruiting officers, and they are to be here with all the boys they can gather, at 3 o'clock, and it's time for them now. Hark! don't you hear them coming?

[*Enter fourteen boys, two with sashes. Corporal Try puts on his sash.*]

JOHN GREEN.—Corporal Try, we have brought to you these boys, who wish to be enrolled as members of your Try Company. I did not happen to have a copy of the rules with me, but if you will read them I think they will all agree to them, for they are boys of the right stamp.

SAMUEL.—Well, boys, I'm glad to have so large an addition to our number, for I hope we shall encourage and help each other. Recruiting officer Brown will read our rules to you.

BROWN.—[*Takes the book, and reads.*] *Rule 1st. When we have anything to do that we ought to do, never say, I* CAN'T.

Rule 2nd. When we have any thing to do that we ought to do, always say, I'LL TRY.

Rule 3rd. When we have anything to do that we ought to do, always do it before play.

Rule 4th. Never do what we are satisfied we ought not to do.

Rule 5th. Never ask anybody else to do what we can do ourselves as well as not.

Rule 6th. Never put off till to-morrow what we can do to-day.

These are our particular rules; but besides these, we have a noble swarm of " Bees," which we call our general rules. They are as follows: Be gentle, Be kind, Be courteous, Be truthful, Be honest, Be diligent.

SAMUEL.—Now, if you agree to these rules, hold up your hands. The Orderly will please enter these names on the record.

[Hiram takes his seat, as Orderly, and the boys call their names in order, as follows :]

1. Archippus Akenside.
2. Barzillai Brighthopes.
3. Chalcedon Champney.
4. Didymus Dotheboy.
5. Entychus Entwistle.
6. Frederic Filchnothing.
7. Gregory Gregorson.
8. Hogarth Harkaway.
9. Ichabod Ireson.
10. Jonathan Jenkinson.
11. Kirk Kickman.
12. Lysander Littleton.

SAMUEL.—You may now assume the badge of our Company, [*passes the badges to each,*] and form a line to receive some visitors that I see approaching. [*Boys hang their badges on their sash.*]

[Enter five large girls, with a banner.]

1st *girl.*—Corporal Try: The young ladies have felt a desire to encourage you in your enterprise, and have therefore prepared a banner, and delegated us to present it to you. I do not know how to make a speech, and so I will tell you a story, and then we will all, if you please, join in singing a song, and I hope this will do instead :—" Farmer Jones had a large field, which he ploughed and planted with corn, and cultivated with great care, hoping to find from it a good support for his family. But after all his work, the corn began to wither and droop for want of rain. He felt very sad and every day he went over and looked at it, and then looked up to see if there was no hope of rain. One day, as he stood looking up, and almost in despair, two little raindrops up in a cloud right over his head, saw him, and one said to the other, ' Look at the poor farmer; I feel sorry for him. He has taken such pains with his field of corn, and now it's all drying up. I wish I could do him some good.' 'Yes,' said the other; but you are only a little raindrop; what can you do? You can't even wet one hillock.' 'Well,' said the first, 'to be sure, I can't do much, but I can cheer the farmer a little, at any rate, and I'm resolved to do my best—I'll try. I'll go down to the field to show my good-will, if nothing more; and so here I go.' And down went the raindrop, and came pat on the farmer's nose. 'Dear me!' said the farmer, putting his finger on his nose, 'what's that? A raindrop! Where did that come from? I do believe we shall have a shower.' No sooner had the first one started, then the second said, 'Well, if you are going, I believe I'll go too; here I come.' And down he dropped on a cornstalk. By this time, a great many raindrops had come together to hear what their companions were talking about, and when they saw them going to cheer the farmer and water the corn, one said, 'If you're going on such a good errand, I'll go too. Look out! Here I come!' 'And I!' said another. 'And I!' 'And I!' 'And I!' and so on, till a whole shower of them came and watered the corn, and it grew and ripened, and all because the first little raindrop determined to do what it could." Now, Corporal, when you and your Company look on this banner, we hope you will keep up good heart, and never be discouraged because you can't do much; for if you do what you can, angels can do no more.

CORPORAL.—We thank you, young ladies, for this expression of your sympathies; and, as you have requested, we will join you in singing.

In strength do we come and in number appear,
  Surrounding our banner with joyful acclaim,
Proclaiming our freedom; no longer we fear,
  No slave to " I can't" shall e'er share in our fame.

Chorus.

The cause that we love, O triumph it must!
With the brave be our motto, " in God is our trust;"

Then long may the Try Comp'ny banner still wave,
"O'er the land of the free and the home of the brave."

In our own land of freedom, be it ever the same,
   Future ages shall read, and rejoice in the story;
Our Try Comp'ny system shall gain us a name,
   And religion shall wreathe our young brows with its glory.

[*Girls retire, bearing the temperance banner.*]

AKENSIDE.—Now, Corporal, Try, I feel pretty good to-day, and I guess we all do, and I propose that we boys go down to the street and procure the material to build a monument on this spot, to commemorate this grand occasion.

LITTLETON.—I second that proposal, for I do believe that we ought to commemorate this occasion. Our fathers celebrate their great days—24th of May, 18th of June, and 1st of July,—and I thing we ought to celebrate the formation of our Try Company—at least, let us raise a monument to-day.

SAMUEL.....Very well, boys; I shall direct the Orderly to lead you, and while you are gone, I wish to persuade James to join us too. [*Company march off in order, under command of Hiram.*] Now, Jemmy, come and join our little band, and see if it won't be a good thing. If you only make up your mind to it, you will find work go easy enough.

JAMES.—Well, Sam, I don't know but I would if I hadn't got such a habit of saying I can't, and knocking things around so. I should forget the rules a dozen times a day, and then mother would say, "There's a pretty member of the Try Company;" and that would make me cross, you know, and I should sulk round worse than ever.

SAMUEL.—Oh, well, never mind. Perhaps it would come rather hard at first, but after a while, you know, you'd learn to say "Try again," and then things would go easy enough.

JAMES.—Well, perhaps I'll join: but you'll have to put me into the awkward squad, I guess, and I hope you won't have a very heavy fine for breaking the rules, for if you do, I shall be dead broke in a short time.

SAMUEL—That's right, Jemmy. [*Hands him a sash, and puts on his own.*] But here come the boys back again, and I should think they meant to have a grand monument.

[*Enter boys as follows: 1st. Hiram as Orderly, and Champney by his side. 2nd. Four boys—Brown, Green, William and Akenside, bearing the base.—3rd, Dotheboy, with a plummet.—4th. Two boys, Entwistle and Filch-nothing, with columns, Industry and Truth.—5th. Bright-hopes, with banner.—6th. Two boys—Gregorson and Hark-away, with columns, Honesty and Courtesy.—7th Two boys—Ireson and Kickman, with the entablature.—8th. Jenkinson, with the cap-stone.—9th, Littleton. The base is laid in its place; the boys with columns, set them down at a little distance from each corner; the entablature and Cap-stone at one side.*]

CHAMPNEY.—Corporal Try, we bring you the base of our monument. On its several sides it bears the mottoes, "Be Gentle," "Be Kind," "Be Merciful," "Be Good." Without the virtues here indicated, we think it impossible to establish a good name among men, and we wish this structure to remind us of all those virtues and principles which should have place in the life of a true Try Company boy.

DOTHEBOY.—[*Tries the base with his plummet.*] I pronounce the base of the monument level and square, and securely laid.

ENTWISTLE.—I propose to place on the north-east angle, the column of Industry, for I know of nothing so necessary to true success in life as indomitable industry. The boy who always has something to do, will always do something. I know that all work and no play makes Jack a dull boy, but I would have every boy industrious at play, and when playtime is over, diligent at his work. [*Places his column.*]

FILCHNOTHING.—I propose for the south-east angle, the column of Truth; for without truthfulness, there can be no real prosperity in anything. The boy that tells a lie, is never to be trusted. As well may we attempt to build our mightiest structures on rotten posts and crumbling columns, as to attempt to build a good character without the support of sound practical truthfulness. [*Places his column.*]

GREGORSON.—I propose the column of Honesty for the north-west angle, because I consider this is one of the indispensable requisites to a sound religious or secular life. There can be no piety where there is no honesty, and there can be no real success in any of the pursuits of life without a sterling integrity of purpose and action. [*Places his column.*]

HARKAWAY.—I ask leave to place the column of Courtesy on the south-west angle, for if we are industrious, honest, and truthful, if we are not affable and courteous we shall do comparatively little to benefit others. Kindness should be an ingredient in all our actions if we would reach a high position in life. [*Places his column.*

IRESON.—Now that we have raised the columns, I wish, with my comrade, to place an entablature on them, bearing on its several sides the mottoes, "Love God," "Love one another," "Love all men," "Love your enemies." These are requirements which are certainly essential to a true life, and which I hope will find expression in the lives of all our comrades. [*The four boys who placed the columns, now place a cricket or covered box at each corner, and help put the entablature in its place.*]

JENKINSON.—I have a cap-stone, on each side of which is the single word, "Grace." I could think of nothing so appropriate, for if all our efforts are not crowned with grace, they will be of little use to us or to anybody else. [*While he is speaking, Jemmy and Dotheboy bring in silently a pair of steps, on which Jenkinson goes up and places his cap-stone in place.*]

KICKMAN.—Now, Mr. Corporal, I move we place upon

the top of our beautiful monument, the banner which our sisters have so kindly presented to us. What place better than this. where its motto may ever be seen, and cheer not only our hearts, but all others who shall see it; and possibly it may in such a position be the means of leading others to join with us, and adopt our principles.

SAMUEL.—Let it be done. [*Ensign mounts the steps, and puts the banner in place.*]

(*Enter four girls, with evergreens, and four with vases of flowers.*)

1ST GIRL.—Corporal Try, we come to adorn your beautiful monunent with evergreens and flowers. We think the occasion demands of us not only the expression of sympathy which our sisters have shown in presenting you with a banner, but we, who are younger than they, can show our interest. We wish, therefore, to wreathe this structure with evergreen, to denote that our sympathies shall ever encircle you in your efforts to do right, and to show yourselves worthy sons of our sires, who dared risk even life in the discharge of duty: [*Each hangs her wreaths on one side of the monument.*]

5TH GIRL.—And we wish, too, in placing these flowers on your monument, to express the desire that the virtues you emulate may ever unfold in you under genial influences from above, as these flowers unfold their beauties under gentle dews and refreshing sunshine. [*Each hands her vase of flowers to a boy, who places it on one corner of the monument.*]

(*Enter a very small girl, with a bouquet of flowers.*)

LITTLE GIRL.—Mr. Corporal I want you to accept this bouquet for yourself. I am a little girl, and can't talk much, but I have learned to say—

'Tis a lesson you should heed,
    Try, try again ;
If at first you don't succeed,
    Try, try again :
Then your courage should appear,
For if you will persevere,
You will conquer, never fear,
    Try, try again.

If you find your task is hard,
          Try, try again ;
Time will bring you its reward,
          Try, try again ;
All that other folks can do,
Why, with patience, may not you ?
Only keep this rule in view—
          Try, try again.

SAMUEL.—We thank you, young ladies, for these ex-
pressions of interest in us; and before you leave us, permit me to ask that you will join us in singing another
song appropriate to this occasion.

Little raindrops feed the rills ;
     Rills to meet the brooklet glide ;
Brooks the broader rivers fill ;
     Rivers swell the ocean's tide.
Thus, the dewdrops gathered here,
     Mites from youthful, willing hands,
Shall those streams of bounty cheer,
     That with greenness clothe the land.

With the sea of love shall blend,
     Which the gospel's grace doth pour,
Till the name of Jesus sound,
     E'en to earth's remotest shore.
Praise to thee, O Lord, forever,
     Gladly now we all unite ;
Praise to thee, O God ! the giver,
     Blessed Lord of life and light !

[*Girls retire.*]

JAMES.—I feel a little ashamed, Corporal, that I refused to help you to do a good deed to-day, but I feel so
much better now, I move we all adjourn to old Rogers,
and do up his work for him without delay.

SAMUEL.—Very well, boys; form line. To the right
face ! Quick—march !

[*All march off in order.*]

MATERIAL OF THE TRY COMPANY.

[The directions here given, may be followed exactly, or modified to suit the taste and circumstances of those who use the piece.]

Eighteen boys, from 12 to 14 years. Six girls, about 12 years. Four girls, about 10 years. Four girls, about 8 years. One girl, about 5 years. Each boy has a sash over right shoulder and under left arm, of blue cambric, bound with white tape, and fastened with a small rosette.

Eighteen badges, with motto, " I'll Try," printed on a card of diamond shape, four inches square, with a loop to hang upon the sash.

A Banner of blue, with motto in gilt letters, " I'll Try." Letters of large size may be cut from gilt paper, and pasted on.

Four evergreen wreaths, 1½ yards long.

Four vases of flowers,

Four covered boxes, about twelve inches high.

Batons for Corporal, Orderly, and Recruiting Officers.

A flight of six steps.

A monument, made as follows;—Base 4 feet square, 16 in high. Four columns, 8 in square, 4 feet high. Entablature 4 ft. square, 8 in high. Cap 2 ft. square, 8 in high. Made of thin boards, not over ⅜ inch in thickness, covered with paper in panels, and with mottoes cut neatly from gilt paper, and pasted on.

In papering the monument, the panels should be of black marble paper, and the outside stiles of plain stone-colored paper, and a narrow moulding of paper between. The columns are draped with pink cambric, and have their mottoes printed on pasteboard, and nailed on.

MY MOTHER'S GOLD RING.

A TEMPERANCE DIALOGUE.

[By a sailor boy, returned from sea, and his brother, from school.]

WILLIAM.—[*Advancing with interest, and taking both his hands.*] Robert, Robert! Is it possible!

ROBERT.—Aye, Willie boy, Robert it is—your own Robin Hood as you loved to call me, when we ranged the wild woods after squirrels, and climbed the tall hickery's to share with them their nuts.

WILLIAM.—Yes, I see your dimple, now you smile. I could pick you out of a thousand little sailor boys, Robin; but how glad I am to see you—glad, indeed, to feel these rough sailors hands in mine.[*Good-naturedly shaking both his hands*]

ROBERT.—Aye, rough they are, for they have seen rough times; but you know nothing about being glad. You must let me say that, for how I have longed for home, and would have given worlds, were they mine, to have flown to you, while I wandered in a land of strangers. Home is home, Willie, be it ever so homely; and although I had but a poor prospect in looking that way, yet I could not help wishing to see you, and mother, and little Jeanette, even though it were in a poor-house, for I felt it would even then comfort my broken-hearted mother only to see me, for it would come sweetly over my mind how poor mother and Jeanette, when they petted me, called me their " little Robin."

WILLIAM.—Sweet Robin, you know it was; but no matter for the by-gones now—you don't know what *good news* I have for you.

ROBERT.—Good news! I wonder which of the four winds can ever blow fair for Bob Luckless, as the sailor called me—for things *would* go wrong—I could not help it. No wonder, Willie, when my heart was all the while away with you ; but when they taunted me, and would say, "*Poor fellow ;* he's thinking of home now ;" I would add, " Avast, you little lubber, with your love knots !" but it was all true, for I would be blurred with tears, hardly knowing what I was about.

WILLIAM.—But you don't ask about your father, Robert.

ROBERT.—Oh, brother ! I feared, I feared to touch that subject—is he then dead ?

WILLIAM—No, Robin Hood, he is *alive* from the dead. [*Embracing him with feeling.*] We have a home, now, and a father, too. Yes, we have a father indeed, and no broken-hearted mother now.

ROBERT.—Can it be true, Willie ? [*Taking his hand, and looking earnestly at him.*] Was it not too much to hope for? What ! is all prosperous and happy again, and have I come in right good season to fill up my mother's cup of joy ?

WILLIAM—Yes, Robin ; and we are back again in the old farm-house, and father has bought the mills.

ROBERT.—Bought the mills ?

WILLIAM.—And the meadow, and the orchard, and the mountain lot, where the mill-pond is.

ROBERT.—What ! the 'Squire's, where we used to skate? Stony Creek meadow, too—what ! all that ?

WILLIAM.—Yes, yes, all father's now ; and Jeanette and I go to school in the village, and have a good time, and mother has the neatest dairy in the country. Mother don't look pale and sad any more ; and Robin, you wouldn't know father, now—no, not at all.

ROBERT.—Happy change ! And is all this in store for Bob Luckless? But tell me, Willie, what has worked this world of wonders ?

WILLIAM.—Sit down here, and I will tell you all, that we may rejoice together at the return of the wanderer— not so much you, dear Robin, but our poor father, who was once lost, but is now found again.

ROBERT.—*That we will rejoice*, for I think lightly of my troubles past, to reach at last so pleasant a port as a peaceful home—but quick, come, tell me all!

WILLIAM.—Well, you remember that dreadful stormy night in October, in which we parted by the big maple-tree at the mill-race, after father turned you out?

ROBERT.—Oh, Willie! don't talk of that now, for my heart bleeds afresh. It must have been a bitter night of troubles for my mother. How often have I heard her say, "I have no comfort, if not in my children." But it is past now.

WILLIAM.—That night, as you know, you went down to Uncle Jones's schooner in the bay.

ROBERT.—Yes, and he received me kindly; and before midnight, with a running gale, we were on the broad ocean. It was a stormy night.

WILLIAM.—But the storm was great at the farm, Robin; for when mother and little Jeanette grieved after you, father beat them, and thrust them both out in that dreadful storm. I stood in the door-way; they reached the bottom of the hill, and mother fell exhausted; then I heard Rover whine, who, poor dog, had followed them as a faithful friend. Returning to the room, all was dark. Father's tempest of rage had past—he was asleep, stretched on the floor. I snatched a few things, closed the doors, and ran with fearful haste to the foot of the hill.

ROBERT.—And poor mother?—

WILLIAM.—Had fainted; and I could not drag little Jeanette away from her. I hastened to neighbor Burns's, and returned with him, found poor Rover, trembling and whining, stretched across them both, as if to keep off the cold storm. Neighbor Burns kindly brought us all to his house.

ROBERT.—Good neighbor Burns! I knew he would do so; honest, sober man—he had his reward in the pleasure of doing it.

WILLIAM.—The old house was stripped of everything next day; father was taken quite ill, to the county poor-house. Mother was some days before she could be moved, and she could follow him, saying to us, "Father shall not want for kind nursing in his sickness." Jeanette and I would not be parted from her, so we all went, and mother nursed him. He was in a few months restored. The winter was severe; I went to work at neighbor Burns's, earned a little daily, and got some comforts for mother, so hope again smiled on us.—But don't you remember, Robin, the little society down at Warwick?

ROBERT.—What, the little cold water company? Yes, I do—I always thought it a good plan for peace and comfort.

WILLIAM.—Well, Charles Wilson spent the holidays at neighbor Burns's. He brought a little green box with his papers, and we all signed and formed a society there. I got a box, too, like Charles's, copied his papers, and got ever so many names, and almost persuaded father, too, for he seemed quite weaned from drink. And he *did sign* at last, as I will soon tell you; and I believe it has saved him and many others from ruin. When father seemed himself again, we went back to the farm house, got a few things together with the help of our neighbors, and we thought all would go well again; but the storm blew back again, and father joined his old companions, and was worse than ever.

ROBERT.—Ah, Willie! that's the way it is at sea. The storm and wind lulls for awhile, then the tempest *bursts* with redoubled fury, tearing all to pieces.—But poor mother?

WILLIAM.—Oh, then she was truly broken-hearted. Hope seemed forever fled. Little Jeanette pined away. At last, a lady kindly took her home; but, though well for Jeanette, it sorely grieved my mother. You know, Robin, father always favored me for I was named after him, and I often persuaded him home, and he would for awhile seem ashamed and sorry; but then again, he would be as hard-hearted as ever, and care for nothing.

ROBERT.—And what, after all, could win him back?

WILLIAM.—There was a soft place in his almost seared conscience, Robin, and it was touched at the right time.

At the close of one of our long tedious days of suffering, mother was wasting away with grief and want, when father had been from home since the night before. I went in search of him, and then, at a late hour of the night, he was among the wicked crowd. I glided close to him, unnoticed. He was reaching his hand to the counter, and something dropped from it to the floor. It was bright and shining, and I knew the little treasure— it was *mother's ring !*

ROBERT.— *What ! mother's gold ring* she used to weep over when she talked of the good times when she first put it on ?

WILLIAM.—It was, Robert. I suddenly took father's hand, looked him kindly in the face, and with a trembling heart, cried "Oh, father, *'Tis mother's gold ring !*" He was for a moment overcome—I led him, weeping, to the door. He was quite himself. We walked silently and sadly home. I told mother what had happened, and and she was strengthened to talk to him. She lifted up her feeble hands to heaven, praying for a blessing on those penitent tears, and those earnest promises. Father seemed as one returning to his senses—was gentle and mild spoken. I ran to my little green box for my temperance pledge, that had all our names on but *his,* and I said, "Come, father let us all be alike, and all one—a whole family in temperance, and perhaps, a whole family in heaven." With a trembling hand, he signed ; then mother, putting the ring on his finger, said, " This shall be a seal of remembrance, William ; look on it, and forgot the past." He then renewed his promises, and what a thankful hour it was, that first hour of peace and rest that mother had known for years. Father was as good as his word, and started next morning early, and threshed all day at neighbor Burns's, and brought his wages to mother at night. Oh, that was a thanksgiving supper, sweetened by the tears of mutual joy and words of peace ; and scanty it was, how truly refreshing, as we experienced how true was the Bible saying, " Better is a dry morsel and a dinner of herbs where love is, than a stalled ox and hatred there-with."

ROBERT.—And has all gone straight since that—no breakers or head winds, Willie?

WILLIAM.—Father continued his orderly conduct. I went daily with him to watch him and pick up a little work with him; and never but once did he turn out of the way by temptation, and then I quickly took his hand, and pointed to the shining treasure on his finger, said, "See father; don't forget *mother's gold ring.*" It was enough; and now it is two years since, and these have been two years of joy and blessing. Father's earnings, and mother's, and sometimes mine, soon laid up a little bank for us; we got a cow, and bought the Stony Brook meadow lot; then one piece of furniture after another bright-ened up our little cottage; the old place began to lift up its head as fast as its master did. The singing birds seemed to rejoice in its groves, and the grass looked greener than ever, and the flowers, two, were sweeter now. Father was at last able to lift the mortage, and bring all back again; little Jeanette returned smiling to a happy home, and all we sighed for was Robin Hood. [*Kindly taking his hand.*]

ROBERT.—And *that* sigh shall be hushed to-night, for I will add one more gladdened heart to the happy family, and give another name to the temperance paper in your little green box, and then all the family, as you say, will indeed be one.

WILLIAM.—What a happy day for all of us and that happiness built on temperance! Only last night it was, when Jeanette lisped your name. "Yes, poor Robin!" said mother; "if he was but here, what more could I wish for? My cup of bliss would then be full."

ROBERT.—So it shall be full and overflowing, too. Mother has all her wishes, and shall sigh no more, and shall never want in days to come, if Robin, the sailor boy, is still spared to her. I have heard wonderful stories, Willie, on the seas, among the sailors, and have heard of wonderful rings in fairy tales, but nothing like the story of Hopewell farm; and no ring like *my mother's gold ring;* and no paper of promise to pay, or payment of sealed deed, like the temperance paper in your little green box, sealed with the tears of penitence and promises of reform. The fame of it shall spread far and wide, wherever Robin the sailor boy goes; and no champion among the knights or giants shall be braver than *he* in the cause of temperance,—or this is not your own Robin Hood who shakes you with his rough hand, Willie, boy. And you shall give *me* the *little green box* with the parchments therein, and every voyage I'll bring it home a yard longer.

WILLIAM.—Then you'll be my own Robin Hood, and mother's own sweet Robin once again.

ROBERT.—Yes, for when I tell the sad, joyful tale of Hopewell farm, I can show father's trembling signature on the paper, and the thoughts of it all cannot fail to touch every heart, and the temperance cause shall always gain by the story of *my mother's gold ring.*

WILLIAM.—So it shall, Robin, for it is a magic ring, indeed. It has healed the broken-hearted, transformed a brute into a man, turned a husband to a loving wife, a father to his children, made a sorrowful house a home of joy and thanksgiving, and has blessed all it touched.

ROBERT.—And the truth of it has touched me, too, Willie, so I shall hoist the temperance flag wherever I sail, teaching the sons of the briny deep to love *fresh water* as they do the waves of their own salt sea, and I trust I shall see the day when many a little green temperance box shall be stowed away in the sailor's till, or the captain's locker, for honest tars are too generous not to give to any cause that will bring relief or comfort to the afflicted, and deliverance to the oppressed. But see—there skips happy little Jeanette, like a little fairy along the lane to the happy farm-house, now to be gladder than ever.

WILLIAM.—Come then, Robin, my sailor boy. [*Taking his hand.*] Let us all sail with this happy breeze of joy into the pleasant port of a temperance home.

...................!

THE VIRTUES.

FOR SIX YOUNG LADIES.

[A personification of six of the principal virtues, by as many young ladies, in the form of a dialogue; 1st, Charity; 2nd, Mercy; 3rd, Humility; 4th, Modesty; 5th, Patience; 6th, Temperance. The young ladies enter, and form a semi-circle. They may dress in costume to suit their tastes. It would be well to give to each a distinct color of dress. Thus: Charity, *white*; Mercy *sky-blue*; Humility, *drab*; Modesty, *pale pink*; Patience, *brown*; Temperance, *green*.]

CHARITY.—Fair sisters, it were fortunate for our fallen race if our dominion were universal.

MERCY.—True, sister Charity, and it would be thy province to warm the world's cold heart, and open the fountain of benevolence, to cause plenty to visit the abodes of penury and want, and drive hunger and misery away.

HUMILITY.—And thine, good sister Mercy, to stay the arm of vengeance, soften the heart of cruelty, plead the cause of the erring, and cause it no longer to be said.

> "Man's inhumanity to man,
> Makes countless thousands mourn."

MODESTY.—And thine, gentle sister Humility, to worship in the ear of the proud, that man is "like the morning cloud and early dew; to check the car of vaulting ambition, and teach pompous vanity to bow at some other than a selfish shrine.

PATIENCE.—And thou, sweet Modesty, daughter of Meekness, art among the brightest relics of Eden! It should be thy province to banish impudence, hold the mirror to the face of egotism, and learn the meritless pretender to see himself as others see him."

TEMPERANCE.—Gladly, quiet sister Patience, should the world hail thee Queen! For thou wouldst drive despondency from the child of affliction, cheer the weary and well-doing, and hold the lamp of hope along the path of enterprise.

CHARITY.—Hail, beautiful sister Temperance! Of all the fair daughters of Virtue there are none whose reign would bless mankind more than thine!

ALL.—Hail, Temperance! Thou art among the fairest and best of the daughters of Virtue!

(The young ladies should pronounce these two lines in full, measured tones in accord.)

CHARITY.—Time, patience and perseverance accomplish all things. Let us, my good sisters, this hour resolve to cease not our efforts until we bring the world under our dominion. Until all the wayward sons of earth shall bow at our shrines, and submit to our peaceful reigns.

ALL.—Most cheerfully, kind sister, do we so resolve, and from this hour will set about the good work.

TEMPERANCE.—I will break the sceptre of old Bacchus, demolish his throne, and banish his *ugly* majesty to the dreary empire of Night, from whence he came. The inebriate shall be clothed in his right mind, bow at the shrine of Temperance, and his sorrowing wife shall cease to lament his folly. I will woo the young from the paths of vice, and cause wisdom to take them by the hand, and lead them along the walks of virtue. The voice of riot shall be hushed, strife and tumult shall cease to wrangle, and reason shall hold universal dominion over the minds of men.

PATIENCE.—I will visit the chamber of affliction, and bid the sufferer hope, will trim the midnight lamp of the student, and point him to the temple of fame, and the chaplet that is weaving for his brow. Mountains shall be removed from the paths of enterprise, the shores of ocean shall shake hands together, and the world shall learn that *patience* and *perseverance* conquer all things. Woman shall contest the palm of science of boasting man, and her brow shall bloom with unfading wreaths, gathered by her own toil from the gardens of literature.

MODESTY.— I will bestow upon woman a brighter gem than ever sparkled in Castalia's fountain. The son of song shall find inspiration in its beams, and the tongue of eloquence glow with rapture in its praise. Modesty shall revive the faded blooms of Eden, and admiring angels. claim again a sisterhood on earth.

HUMILITY.—I will teach the proud to become as little children, and the boasting to bow meekly at the feet of wisdom, and learn the vanity of earthly possessions; will point them to the heavens and the earth, to the vast suns that blaze, beautiful stars that twinkle, and stupendous comets that revolve through the wide empire of space, and ask them what is man that he should boast when the vain oppressor is revelling in his hall, receiving the flatteries of dependents, and dreaming of an increase of power and magnificence, I will startle him from his dreams by writing in mysterious characters upon the wall: "Thou art weighed in the balance and found wanting;" thy throne is tottering to ruins, and liberty is now preparing thy grave, oh, tyrant.

MERCY.—I will remind man that Heaven was merciful to him, when the flaming sword of justice would have cut him down, and therefore to be merciful to his fellows. I will stand by the side of the judge, and mysteriously incline the scale to the side of mercy rather than of vengeance: and will visit the gloomy prison-house, unbar its massive doors, and unclose the chains of the fettered. The strong shall cease to oppress the weak, and the obdurate heart of cruelty shall be melted into tenderness.

CHARITY.—And I will not be idle, fair sisters. I will

dry up the tears of the sorrowing one, hush the cry of the orphan for bread, cause the rose of plenty to bloom upon the pale cheek of want, and illuminate the desolate dominions of misery with the smiles of hope.

ALL.—Hail, sister Charity, brightest star that illuminates our fallen earth, may universal dominion soon be thine. And may this intelligent audience fall in love with Charity, Mercy, Humility, Modesty, Patience and Temperance, and submit to their happy reigns.

(*Curtain drops as the ladies all clasp hands and form in a circle. around* CHARITY *as if to crown her.*)

THE OLD LADY'S WILL.

[These several characters should dress in costume becoming their callings. When well rendered, the scene is very humorous.]

Characters.

SQUIRE DRAWL.   FRANK MILLINGTON.

SWIPES, a brewer.   CURRIE, a saddler.

(Enter SWIPES *and* CURRIE.)

SWIPES.—A sober occasion this, brother Currie! Who would have thought the old lady was so near her end?

CURRIE.—Ah! we must all die, brother Swipes. Those who live longest outlive the most.

SWIPES.—True, true; but since we must die and leave our earthly possession, it is well that the law takes such good care of us. Had the old lady her senses when she departed?

CURRIE.—Perfectly, perfectly. Squire Drawl told me she read every word of her last will and testament aloud, and never signed her name better.

SWIPES.—Had you any hint from the squire what disposition she made of her property?

CURRIE.—Not a whisper! the squire is as close as a miser's purse. But one of the witnesses hinted to me that she had cut off her graceless nephew with a shilling.

SWIPES.—Has she? Good soul! Has she? You know I come in, then, in right of my wife.

CURRIE.—And I in my *own* right, and this is no doubt, the reason why we have been called to hear the reading of the will. Squire Drawl knows how things should be done, if he is as air-tight as one of your own beer barrels, brother Swipes. But here comes the young reprobate. He must be present, as a matter of course, you know. (*Enter* FRANK MILLINGTON.) Your servant, young gentleman. So, your benefactress has left you, at last!

SWIPES.—It is a painful thing to part with old and good friends, Mr. Millington.

FRANK.—It is so, sir; but I could bear her loss better, had I not so often been ungrateful for her kindness. She was my only friend, and I knew not her value.

CURRIE.—It is too late to repent, Master Millington. You will now have a chance to earn your own bread.

SWIPES.—Ay, ay, by the sweat of your brow, as better people are obliged to do. You would make a fine brewer's boy, if you were not too old.

CURRIE.—Ay, or a saddler's lackey, if held with a tight rein.

FRANK.—Gentlemen, your remarks imply that my aunt has treated me as I deserved. I am above your insults, and only hope you will bear your fortune as modestly, as I shall mine, submissively. I shall retire. (*As he is going, enters* SQUIRE DRAWL.)

SQUIRE.—Stop, stop, young man! We must have your presence. Good morning, gentlemen; you are early on the ground.

CURRIE.—I hope the Squire is well to-day.

SQUIRE.—Pretty comfortable for an invalid.

SWIPES.—I trust the damp air has not affected your lungs.

SQUIRE.—No, I believe not. You know I never hurry, *Slow and sure* is my maxim. Well, since the heirs-at-law are all convened, I shall proceed to open the last will and testament of your deceased relative, according to law.

SWIPES.—(*While the* SQUIRE *is breaking the seal.*) It is a trying scene to leave all one's possessions, Squire, in this manner!

CURRIE.—It really makes me feel melancholy when I look round and see every thing but the venerable owner of these goods. Well did the preacher say, "All is vanity!"

SQUIRE.—Please to be seated, gentlemen. (*All sit. The* SQUIRE *puts on his spectacles, and reads slowly.*) "Imprimis: Whereas my nephew, Francis Millington, by his disobedience and ungrateful conduct, has shown himself unworthy of my bounty, and incapable of managing my large estate, I do hereby give and bequeath all my houses, farms, stocks, bonds, moneys, and property, both personal and real, to my dear cousins, Samuel Swipes, brewer, and Christopher Currie, saddler." [SQUIRE *takes off his spectacles to wipe them.*]

SWIPES.—(*Dreadfully overcome.*) Generous creature! kind soul! I always loved her.

CURRIE.—She *was* good, she *was* kind! She was in her right mind. Brother Swipes, when we divide, I think I will take the mansion house.

SWIPES.—Not so fast, if you please, Mr. Currie! My wife has long had her eye upon that, and must have it.

[*Both rise.*

CURRIE.—There will be two words to that bargain, Mr Swipes! And, besides, I ought to have the first choice. Did not I lend her a new carriage every time she wished to ride? And who knows what influence—

SWIPES.—Am I not named first in her will! And did I not furnish her with my best small beer for more than six months? And who knows what influence—

FRANK.—Gentlemen I must leave you. [*Going.*

SQUIRE.—(*Wiping his spectacles and putting them on.*) Pray gentlemen, keep your seats. I have not done yet. (*All sit.*) Let me see; where was I?—Ay,—"All my property, both personal and real, to my dear cousin, Samuel Swipes, brewer—

SWIPES.—Yes!

SQUIRE.—"And Christopher Currie, saddler—"

CURRIE.—Yes!

SQUIRE.—"To have and to hold, IN TRUST, for the sole and exclusive benefit of my nephew, Francis Millington, until he shall have attained the age of twenty-one years; by which time I hope he will so far have reformed his evil habits, as that he may safely be intrusted with the large fortune which I hereby bequeath to him."

SWIPES.—What's all this? You don't mean that we are humbugged? *In trust!*—how does that appear? Where is it?

SQUIRE.—(*Pointing to the parchment.*) There! In two words of as good old English as I ever penned.

CURRIE.—Pretty, well, too, Mr. Squire, if we must be sent for to be made laughing-stocks of! She shall pay for every ride she had out of my chaise, I promise you!

SWIPES.—And for every drop of my beer. Fine times, if two sober, hard-working citizins are to be brought here to be made the sport of a graceless profligate! But we will manage his property for him, Mr. Currie! We will make him feel that trustees are not to be trifled with!

CURRIE.—That will we!

SQUIRE.—Not so fast, gentlemen; for the instrument is dated three years ago, and the young gentleman must already be of age and able to take care of himself. Is it not so, Francis?

FRANK.—It is. [*Exit, laughing.*

SQUIRE.—Then, gentlemen, having attended to the breaking of this seal according to law, you are released from any further trouble in the premises.]

[*Exeunt in anger*, SQUIRE *laughing*